WHO'S WITH US?

WHO'S

FROM WONDERING TO KNOWING IF YOU

WITH

SHOULD START A BUSINESS IN 21 DAYS

US?

BY ANGELA LUSSIER

AUTHOR OF THE ANTI-RESUME REVOLUTION

Table of Contents

Introduction

Sitting in a coffee shop, I thoroughly inspect each person as he or she enters. I imagine each person's life, starting with what inspired them to come in and order their double shot, extra creamy, extra sweet, extra iced, double mochaccino latte. I wonder what their days are like, what struggles they have, what keeps them up at night, and if their mind also wanders like mine when they try to get something important done. Am I the only one with this problem? Am I the only one who sets a goal to accomplish something and then looks around the room for distractions and reasons not to start?

The truth is, I encountered so much internal resistance while writing this book that I should have started calling this project The NeverEnding Story (but the title was already taken). At first, I was a rock star, writing two to three hours each day for an entire month. When I finished the first draft on Day 30, I printed out my manuscript. As soon as I saw it in broad daylight, I looked at it like it was my newborn baby I didn't really want anymore. In return, this baby was looking at me like I was the alien. The complicated relationship with the book had just begun.

Our first meeting, July 8, 2014

I shoved my unwanted baby into an envelope and drove it to my editor's office. As soon as he opened the door, he could tell something was up. My face was expressionless. I mean, "poker-faced" does not even begin to describe me at this point. My mind was empty except for the deep, dark thoughts that wanted me to know this book might be terrible and I was making a huge mistake.

He gave me a pep talk, and I fought back tears until I made it to the protection of my car. Once I pulled out into the crowded street and safe zone of anonymity, I let it rip. Tears streamed from my eyes like a garden hose watering the lawn after a heat wave. I let out a loud wail. All the fears I had about being seen, being judged, and being a terrible writer flowed out of me. This cleansing freak show lasted the entire twenty-minute drive back to my office. Getting out of my car, I couldn't escape the sinking feeling that in deciding to write this book, I had made a big mistake.

If you are an artist, writer, creative professional, entrepreneur, or have ever set out to do something risky, you are most likely laughing right now or commiserating with my teary commute and fear of putting myself out there. You know what it's like to finish something you've poured your heart into, something you created because you felt you had to. You know how it feels to want to run away with your tail between your legs once the thought of other people seeing your work becomes reality. The tricky thing about creativity is that the opposite side of the coin is fear: your fear that something made from your heart and soul could be wrong, bad, boring, misunderstood, or, worst of all, ignored. Fighting through this fear and doing it anyway is what it takes to be in business. Not everyone is born with this ability. Some cultivate the strength while others quit. Learning which type of person you are is what you will learn in this book and will help you determine whether or not starting a business is for you.

My Story

Hi, I'm Angela.

Over the last six years as a career and business coach, I've presented to thousands of questioning careerists and sat across the table from hundreds of aspiring business owners, ambitious dreamers, and fearful professionals who want to venture out on their own but don't think they have the chops to do so. Through helping them go from stifled and unfulfilled to growing and creating, I can tell you for a fact that the process of creating a business is not merely a mechanical one. You can read a book about how to write a business plan, learn how to ask for funding from a bank, and research how to apply for patents, but the real secret to doing the work and making your vision come to life lies in the stories you tell yourself, the beliefs you have about who you are, and the way you manage the limitations you impose on yourself. As the process of venturing out on your own unfolds, you start to question your abilities, your knowledge, and your aptitude. You may also start to wonder whether or not you are a good business person, sales person or people person. The questions become endless. It's what you do with the questions that will determine how far you make it in the land of self-employment.

After listening to my clients and workshop participants ask the same questions over and over, I knew I needed to create something that would answer those questions: "Should *I* start a business?", "What if it doesn't work?", and "How will I know if I made the right choice?" Recognizing that my conversations with clients followed several easily identifiable patterns, writing this book felt more like a calling than an idea.

The Lesson

What I've found out about myself and observed in thousands of others is that the road to business ownership is an amazing, and yes, harrowing exercise in self-reflection, self-awareness, and self-care. As you read this book, you will be asked to challenge your assumptions about what business means to you, to ask yourself questions about what you want from this journey, and to start putting the pieces together to build your mission. The process is an internal one that has more to do with you, the business owner, than the customer, the product, the office space, and the marketing. You are the Wizard of Oz, the President, the General and the Master of your Universe. You get to build a business and since you are the captain of the ship, you need to know where you are going and what tools you have to get you there. It's a big responsibility, but it's also an exciting opportunity to share your talents, gifts, and creative eye in ways you may have only dreamt of. Woah!

Join Us

As the title of this book implies, taking on the possibility of business ownership means you are joining a league of risk takers who are putting it all on the line. In doing so, you will forge new friendships, think differently about what work means to you, and see the act of being paid for your work in an entirely new way. You will be stepping out of the rat race and into a lifestyle you get to design. By answering the call, "Who's with us?" you will be determining once and for all, if you are in for the great journey of self-employment, or if the dream was merely just that – and you are destined for greatness somewhere else.

The Ask

There is a lot to consider, but you don't have to figure it all out today. Read this book with open eyes, an open mind, and an open heart. Everything will unfold and open up to you if you pay attention, start doing the work, and don't give up. It's a process. You will cry. It will be hard. You will think you're crazy. (You're not...well, maybe a little). Be brave and know that this is an experiment, like everything else you do. Join me. Sign up for the adventure. Change your life, even if you're not ready. The truth is, no one is ever "ready." Not you. Not me.

Let's do it anyway.

Angela Lussier
Holyoke, Massachusetts
July 1, 2015

Dedication:

For Nick, Gratitude, and Lilly

CHAPTER 1

Your Map

"We're different. I can't do this anymore."

I was trembling with fear, but I did my best to hide it by speaking quickly. My only goal going into the meeting: do not, under any circumstances, stay at this job.

As I said the words, I wondered how they were being received. To me, they sounded like a train hitting a brick wall, or perhaps something you would say to end a long-term relationship rather than employment.

I was always the idea person, the one who wanted to create change and try new things. I worked late and poured myself into my work. This didn't always go over well and was one of the major sources of frustration for me because I loved to solve problems, look at what could improve, and question the big picture. These attributes, coupled with the fact that I realized I was wasting my time and talent in endless staff meetings and pointless company retreats, were some of the major reasons I started considering working for myself.

I didn't like the person I was when I got swept up in break-room gossip. I felt sick from working in poorly decorated and poorly lit cubicle spaces. Abiding by employee handbooks with things like "release time" for doctor's appointments became the bane of my existence. Participating in never-ending performance reviews, with no promise of anything in exchange for a job well done, was a particular problem for me. I knew if I didn't do something about it, I would be living a miserable existence forever. Recognizing that I was no longer a "company woman" was the first step in realizing there was a whole other world out there waiting for me: self-employment. This world looked like a dream come true. No annoying co-workers who don't get their work done on time? No time clock or work schedule? No awkward birthday parties in the break room? The more I explored this option, the more I knew being the boss of my own company was the life I was meant to live. The only question was, How? That question became easier for me to answer as I grew wearier of the 9-5 lifestyle. I knew that if I had one more boss tell me I needed to be at work on time (for no particular reason) or that my outfit didn't meet the (unnecessary) dress code, I was going to show a side of myself no one wanted to see. There was a small-yet-very-smart part of me deep down that kept saying I was meant for bigger things. Telling this story sounds a bit like folklore in that there isn't one thing I can point to that gave me the confidence or belief that starting a business would work for me. It was more like a risk I was ready to take because I already knew the alternative and I knew it wasn't for me.

Twenty minutes after I quit, I walked out of the office a free woman. I was fueled by rage and 10 years of pent-up creativity. I was overflowing with ideas I was never given the opportunity to use. The uncertainty, the questioning, and an even bigger fear of the unknown would come, but they weren't important to me in that moment. What mattered was that I was in control for the first time. I had no more barriers and no more time to waste. I launched my business as soon as I got home.

March 30, 2009, became known as Day 1. It was the day I restarted everything and never looked back. I started a career consulting firm and began reading business books and blogs, attending seminars, getting advice from other business owners, and scheduling business counseling sessions with advisors. I learned the mechanics of business, like how to make a Profit & Loss Statement, how to make a business plan, and which networking groups existed in the area. In all of the information and advice I received, some helpful, some not so much, there was a huge chunk of information missing. No one really wanted to talk about the side that is dark, unknown, confusing, scary and could stop a hopeful business owner in their tracks: what I call the *other* side of the startup. I had to figure this all out on my own and it was not at all like I expected.

Why I Am Writing This Book

I remember the first time a client finished a session by slamming her laptop closed and said, "I wish I had met you ten years ago. You saved me more time and worry than I can ever express to you." I remember it because that was the moment I had been searching for since I quit the corporate world. The feeling was like a drug and I became hooked on helping others find or create work they loved.

As I've learned more about my industry and the resources that exist for aspiring business owners, I've noticed a conversation that is often left out: the business owner's personal journey. This is the emotional and mental ordeal of putting it all on the line. There are many books about sales strategies, setting goals, competitive analysis, and marketing, but where are the books that help you anticipate what your life will become when you decide to leave the comfort of a paycheck and go all in with a new business?

Once I recognized there wasn't a good book to recommend (or a crisis hotline), my decision to write this book was easy. The actual *doing* part was a whole different story. And here lies the story of the business owner. Big dreams, big goals, and big ideas are constant. Where we get tripped up is getting our ideas off the ground. This book is all about the personal side of starting a business: what the business owner goes through in order to make their ideas into products and services, say to the world "Here I am," and truly go for it. What I've observed over and over again is that success isn't all about having the right product and doing the best marketing. It's about you. It's about your habits, your beliefs, and your stories. Addressing these areas is what you'll learn in this book.

Why You Are Reading This Book

You have an idea for a business, but you're not certain how to bring it into the world. You've rolled it around, you've run it by a few friends, you've trolled around the internet to see if it already exists… maybe you've even procrastinated (a little). The idea eats away at you when your boss is on a rampage or you sit in commuter traffic and realize you are wasting time. You daydream and you wonder, "Should I, could I, start a business?" By the end of this book, you will have the answer to this question. Should you decide business ownership is for you, I have written a second book which teaches how to go about starting your very own business.

What This Book Is

This book is a manual for aspiring business owners who feel frustrated and unable to take action despite having asked themselves big, important questions. This book will help you find answers. This book is also much like the meetings I hold with my clients. It's a time and space to reflect, inquire, and consider different possibilities so you can address all the pieces that will go into building your business. Think of this as a guidebook where you set a destination and prepare to embark on your journey. My goal is to give you every tool you need to decide if business ownership is truly where you want to go, and if so, how to get started right away. If you decide business ownership is not for you, then this book has also served its purpose.

This book is broken down into thirteen chapters, ten exercises, and one quiz to help you assess whether or not you are ready to start a business. Many of the chapters will require self-reflection and inquiry into a variety of topics such as beliefs, passions, values, and even business skills, like sales. The last exercise is a self-assessment which brings all your work together to give you the answer to your biggest question: "Should I start a business?"

What This Book Is Not

If you decide at some point during the book that business ownership is not for you, and it's clear that finding a new job is the right step, this book will not teach you how to find a job. However, my first book, *The Anti-Résumé Revolution*, will.

How to Read This Book

Get a notebook. Get a highlighter and a pen. Prepare some Post-It pads or bookmarks to keep track of the questions you need to follow up with or exercises you need to revisit. This is a manual that walks you through all of the steps and topics you need to address before getting started. It's meant to be read in order, as each chapter builds from the last. The first thing you should do is download your very own Personal Escape Plan workbook from my website. This is where you will keep track of your findings from each exercise so you have your conclusions, questions, and action steps in one place. Additional copies of all the worksheets and additional resources are available for download on my website, *www.domakebusiness.com* under the Book tab. Enter the password DoItAnyway to get access.

This book also includes stories from many other business owners who arrived at the same point I did in 2009—they had enough and needed out. I encourage you to check out their websites and see what they have built as a result of leaving their jobs and starting their own businesses. Their expertise ranges from financial advising and restaurant ownership to manufacturing and photography. Note the stories you like, the advice you want to remember, and business models that resonate with you. By the time you finish reading the book, you will have a business diary of your thoughts, ideas, and goals. You'll even have a plan for how to make them live and breathe.

Who's With Us?

"Who's With Us?" refers to that moment when you decide to leave your job and pursue the unknown along with the business owners I feature in this book and millions of others. When you step out of the rat race and decide you no longer want to trade precious hours of your life for a pension and a cubicle, you will start to feel a kinship with others who have made the same choice. The deep connection you will feel to other visionaries who decided to stop hiding and start living will enrich your life and give your journey an even stronger meaning.

I urge you to complete this book in 21 days, as the subtitle suggests. The exercises are meant to build on one another, but not all in one day. There needs to be time for reflection in between each one while also maintaining momentum and focus. At the end of 21 days, you should have done enough work to determine whether or not you are destined to own your own business.

Ready or not…

CHAPTER 2

You Are Not Alone

There's a moment that comes in almost every initial coaching session when I have to hold back laughter. This inevitable moment comes when my client expresses his or her fear of being weird for wanting to leave a comfortable job to do something "crazy." They have no idea how many people feel exactly the same way! From new beginners to seasoned pros, many people are weighing the same questions and want the same things. They (and likely you) just haven't found them yet.

I'll give a classic example. I had one client who referred to herself as "Whack Job" for our first three sessions. She had convinced herself she was insane for wanting to leave a steady paycheck to pursue her dream of opening a marketing firm. She had an excellent track record at her job and was in a stable industry. Chances of being laid off were close to zero percent and she was well respected by her colleagues and managers. Her friends and family couldn't understand why she would give that up for something risky and unknown. After continuing to work with her, she did leave her job, stopped calling herself a whack job, and is still in business today. She came to realize that just because she wasn't taking the typical path, it didn't mean there was anything wrong with her! In this chapter, you'll read several stories from people like her you so you can start erasing your fear about your journey being a solo one. Many have taken this path before, many are on it right now, and many more will do it in the future. Don't worry that no one understands—I do, and so do your fellow dreamers, some of whom you will meet in the pages to come.

~~~

Prior to becoming a full-time professional artist, Robyn Spady was Director of Marketing and Communications for a high-tech consulting company near Seattle. In July 1999, she finally achieved a corporate American status symbol—the corner office with a conference table. On a Monday morning, she moved into her new office, set up her rosewood furniture, and gazed over Lake Washington. Two days later, she looked up from her desk, surveyed the office, and thought, "This is it?" She had never before felt so unfulfilled by achieving a goal. She experienced a tremendous feeling of letdown and disappointment. These feelings are not uncommon, and they often occur when a major event doesn't live up to the vision created by the imagination. Robyn likened it to several moments we all anticipate. Becoming a parent for the first time and feeling overwhelmed with responsibility. Getting married and having the wedding behind and realizing you're no longer the center of attention. Buying your first house only to feel how ominous it is to be in debt more than ever.

While she had achieved a career goal, she realized the corporate America dream was, for her, merely a delusion. She says, "With a career, I had an expectation that my achievements would lead to feeling success and that all of the time and effort put in would be rewarding, as though my contributions and accomplishments would make a difference in my contribution to the world around me." Instead, she felt, well, nothing. When she realized her dream of "being somebody" no longer mattered, she knew she had to make a change.

Planning her exit was not simple or quick since she had adapted her lifestyle to a certain income level. However, her timing was fortunate; the high-tech bubble bursting in 2000 hit her company right away. To save money, the senior executives decided to downsize. The biggest bang-for-the-buck was to eliminate all of the directors in a single day. And so, January 2001, Robyn was given three choices: 1) return to consult for the company, 2) lay off one of her managers, or 3) choose voluntary layoff. Given her many doubts about corporate life, few decisions had been easier for her. She went with option #3. Robyn now owns and runs Spady Studios, a hand-weaving resource for artists and enthusiasts.

Robyn's story may be similar to yours in that you also feel unfulfilled, yet trapped, by your job. Many people are like Robyn—not interested in the corner office, but instead interested in working on their own terms and without the constraints of a formal work environment. According to Entrepreneur.com[1], around 600,000 businesses are started each year in the United States. See, you're not alone at all. In fact, you may be joining the growing ranks of the self-employed without even realizing it.

Another stomach-churning worry you may be facing is a lack of opportunities to use your creativity. But fear not! Boredom is an indispensable litmus test and a powerful catalyst for change. Consider the story of Tammy Gunn. Before she started her business, she had multiple jobs ranging from doctor's assistant to office manager. While riding the bus to work one day, she couldn't deny the disappointment she felt having to sit at a desk for another day. Spending eight hours typing and answering phones didn't make sense to her anymore. A change had occurred inside of her and she said enough was enough. She describes that day as the longest, and by the end of it, she had written out on a piece of paper "I WILL RUN MY OWN BUSINESS!" Tammy now owns the Live Out Loud Movement, a Zumba and laughter yoga studio in Toronto.

In the stories throughout this book, you'll notice no one decided to leave their job because they were "supposed to," which is often the terminology used when describing one's climb up the corporate ladder, or rationalizing staying at the same terrible job too long. When Karin Hurt, an executive at Verizon for twenty years, decided she wanted a new challenge, she took action. During her last three years of employment, she was juggling a quickly growing leadership blog and speaking circuit with her

---

1 From *Starting a Business: The Idea Phase*: http://www.entrepreneur.com/article/217368

extremely demanding day job. The exhilaration that came with her new endeavor became hard to resist, and she began waking up early to rush to her computer and see what her email would bring. Karin says, "I felt alive and full of meaning with the growing connections of kindred spirits and leaders needing support." This feeling of excitement was what propelled her to quit her corporate job and move into self-employment full-time.

Conversely, some people didn't need an unsatisfying job to instigate a change. They were looking for an escape from the rest of their confusing life. Cody McLain, owner of MindHack.com, was only fifteen when he discovered the benefits of starting a business. When he and a friend wanted to raise money to buy an X-Box, they learned how to resell web-hosting services through an existing hosting company. Cody says, "During the first week I found a tremendous passion in building something that I knew would be a great challenge." Being only fifteen, he faced other challenges, like opening a checking account to accept payments and figuring out credit card processing. "I'd come home after school every day and just worked straight into the night; learning everything from managing a business to coding html," explains Cody. He dealt with screaming customers, server crashes, hackers, and utter disasters. Cody says, "I realized, though, I was lucky. I was lucky to have found something I'm good at and enjoy."

Stories like these continue throughout the entire book. While reading, pay attention to what rings true for you and how each business owner's insight could help you make your decision. Remember, you're not alone—you are one of many people who have contemplated the same questions, same worries, and same plans for venturing out on your own. So, I'll ask you now and I'll ask you again at the end of this book:

Who's With Us?

CHAPTER 3

External Influences: What to Do about Your Cranky Boss

DAY 1

Ready to dig deep? In the pages to come, you will have the opportunity to focus on several different parts of your work world in order to better understand what you want. For now, we're going to address what's bothering you, determine what you can and cannot change, and start making a plan for your next steps. I break down the two types of influences, internal and external, into separate chapters so you can see clearly where your feelings, both positive and negative, are coming from. This chapter focuses on external influences, which are factors largely out of your control such as your boss, your co-workers, your work schedule, and the company culture you face every day. These factors affect your happiness, success, and feeling of accomplishment.

If you agree with any of these statements, you are going to love the rest of this chapter:

- I work with a bunch of amateurs who can't get their act together.
- My boss is out to get to me and is squashing my potential.
- For the amount of crap I put up with, I should be making a lot more money.
- I don't even want to add up how much time I waste during my daily commute.
- If I keep this up, I'm going to burn out in five years.

Do these statements sound like something you'd say? One of the most damaging aspects of this thought cycle is that even though it deals with external problems, it lives inside of you like a worm and can start to eat away at your self-confidence, which in turn erodes your ability to see other options.

How often do you voice these concerns? How often do you seek other possibilities rather than live in this predicament? Constantly questioning a bad situation can become a part of life. You start to be comfortable in the discomfort because you're used to it, maybe it becomes too hard to change or—worse—you're afraid of the unknown so you do nothing.

Get Out of Your Head

One of my favorite things to tell my clients is this: the best thing you can do for yourself is get out of your head. Chances are, you've had the same upsetting thoughts every day for months, maybe even years, and every time you ask yourself what you should do, you come up with the same answer (or no answer at all). Getting caught up in your own internal drama is a sure-fire way to stay stuck. If you want to change your thoughts, change your behavior. Reading this book and completing the exercises are a great way to get out of your head and start putting a plan in place. In addition, try asking other people what they did when they felt this way. Instead of saying to yourself, "My boss is out to get to me," ask someone, "Have you ever worried that your boss didn't have your best interests at heart? What did you do about it?" Sometimes, hearing other people's stories will give you new ways to look at your situation and they may even inspire you to take action.

Maybe you've worked for the boss who feels he is on the same level as Alexander the Great or the Pope. Whatever he says is unquestionable truth. You've been marginalized, criticized, and put in your place more times than you can count, and you wonder why you still allow yourself to be treated this way. When Marc Renson was working as the food production manager for a state university in New York, he encountered a boss with a God complex. After being verbally threatened, harassed, and assaulted by flying objects, he decided to report the behavior. His boss was required to take anger management classes, which only made him more difficult to deal with. After enduring several more months of hellish conditions, Marc says, "On January 18th, 2000, I walked into work and submitted my on-the-spot resignation letter the same day 30,000 students came back from winter break. I walked out with guns blazing and never looked back!" Marc now owns Ambition Bistro in Schenectady, New York.

I can empathize with Marc's story. One of the less enjoyable jobs I had included an explosive boss, priorities that shifted daily, and unclear goals. Putting my energy into projects that never saw the light of day, feeling confused by the vision of the leadership, and being told almost weekly "I'm disappointed in you" by my boss was beyond frustrating and irritating. Because I was a less experienced member of the team, my ideas were not made a legitimate part of the conversation and, therefore, I felt small and useless. What drove me crazy was the fact that I was so young and already miserable at work. I often asked myself if this was what my career would be like forever.

Of course, my story and Marc's story have been experienced by thousands, perhaps millions of people. Like us, Elizabeth Fife of New York City realized she was too young to hate her job. Her unhappy situation motivated her to think about doing something else. After spending three good years helping private companies raise money through her investment banking position, she decided to try a new job in finance only to find a completely different experience. Elizabeth's new boss was a nightmare. On top of that, she didn't care about what she was doing and she dreaded getting up every morning. It wasn't until she was asked to interview new candidates to work for her when she realized she didn't care enough about finance to give her life to it. Elizabeth says, "I felt that I was too young to hate my job. I was so fortunate that I had the support of my friends and mainly my parents to then try opening my own business." Leaving pie charts and PowerPoint behind, Elizabeth set out to develop a new and exciting alternative dessert. After scouring bakeries and employing a team of recipe testers, Elizabeth launched Batter & Cream, an online bakery that delivers whoopie pies in gourmet flavors.

Sometimes, in a toxic situation, it can be hard to see how bad things have become because you get used to them. Being yelled at can seem normal and a lack of respect becomes ordinary. When you decide you're worth more and you deserve more, that's when change can happen. When Chris Landry of Northampton, Massachusetts, was sick of not being recognized for his hard work, he decided to do something about it. After a twenty-year career in the non-profit world, he had amassed a strong set of skills and built a reputation as someone who could get the job done. He grew used to a culture of organizational politics and dysfunction until the day he made a significant contribution that went unnoticed. Chris says, "I had written a successful $5 million grant proposal and saw someone else receive (and take) all the credit. It wasn't about ego, it was about being part of an organization that somehow hadn't noticed I worked thirty straight days, eight to ten hours a day, writing and rewriting a brilliant proposal that won against long odds." This snub was the last straw. Rather than wait around, he asked his boss to lay him off so he could get out to do his own thing. Looking back on it, Chris reflects, "Working for people who can't see how much you contribute is like staying in a bad relationship; it feels bad and it's just not healthy." Chris now owns Landry Communications, a firm that helps companies, NGOs and foundations work to create a more just and sustainable world. His firm is now thriving, although he says, "It wasn't easy, and I struggled to find my way. I saw that I needed to commit to a specific niche so I went with my strengths and my passion. I love the challenge and the rewards of what I'm doing."

So, What's Bothering You?

In the following worksheet, we will look at the external influences that can affect your happiness and satisfaction at work. This exercise will help you see which of these areas are bothering you and motivating you to make a change. If you learn that all of your unhappiness is centered on your boss, maybe starting a business isn't what you really want; instead, you should be seeking a new gig with a strong leadership team. If you find that having a boss—any boss—is a problem for you, getting a new job probably won't make you happy. Being your own boss might.

The HAM Method

A strategy I developed is called the HAM Method, and it works well for evaluating the external influences you are facing. "H" stands for "Headache," "A" stands for "Adjust," and "M" stands for "Map." For any given issue you will be given the opportunity to ask yourself three questions to assess your situation:

- Is this giving me a <u>headache</u>?
- Is this something I can <u>adjust</u>?
- If so, what does my <u>map</u> look like?

Answering these questions will determine where your unhappiness lies and can help you understand your options. The thing to remember is that any frustrations or regrets you have today are totally reversible and within your control. By breaking down what is bothering you, you will be able to clearly see what to fix and how to move forward. These areas are important to address now so you have a baseline to work from as you go through the rest of the book and wrestle with some of the biggest decisions you will ever make.

Go to www.domakebusiness.com/book and enter the password DoItAnyway to download this worksheet.

BONUS: Download your Personal Escape Plan workbook to keep track of your findings from each of the worksheets to come!

WORKSHEET #1: EVALUATION OF NOW— EXTERNAL INFLUENCES

To fill this out, use the HAM Method (Headache, Adjust, Map) to dig deep. Here is an example of how this would look:

CATEGORY:

Your Pay

Is this giving me a headache? Yes. I have not had a raise in two years even though I have been promised one several times.

Is this something I can adjust? Not at my current company, but if I looked for a new job or started my own business, yes.

If so, what does my map look like? I will set a termination date with my employer and start considering whether or not a new job or a new business is best.

CATEGORIES:

YOUR BOSS

Is this giving me a headache? _____
_____
_____

Is this something I can adjust?_____
_____
_____

If so, what does my map look like? _____
_____
_____

CO-WORKERS

Is this giving me a headache? _____
_____
_____

Is this something I can adjust?_____
_____
_____

If so, what does my map look like? _____
_____
_____

YOUR PAY

Is this giving me a headache? _____
_____
_____

Is this something I can adjust?_____
_____
_____

If so, what does my map look like? _____
_____
_____

BENEFITS

Is this giving me a headache? _____
_____
_____

Is this something I can adjust?_____
_____
_____

If so, what does my map look like? _____
_____
_____

THE JOB ITSELF

Is this giving me a headache? _____

_____

_____

Is this something I can adjust?_____

_____

_____

If so, what does my map look like? _____

_____

_____

WORK SCHEDULE

Is this giving me a headache? _____

_____

_____

Is this something I can adjust?_____

_____

_____

If so, what does my map look like? _____

_____

_____

COMMUTE

Is this giving me a headache? _____

_____

_____

Is this something I can adjust?_____

_____

_____

If so, what does my map look like? _____
_____
_____

UPWARD MOBILITY

Is this giving me a headache? _____
_____
_____

Is this something I can adjust?_____
_____
_____

If so, what does my map look like? _____
_____
_____

RECOGNITION

Is this giving me a headache? _____
_____
_____

Is this something I can adjust?_____
_____
_____

If so, what does my map look like? _____
_____
_____

COMPANY CULTURE

Is this giving me a headache? _____
_____
_____

Is this something I can adjust?_____
_____
_____

If so, what does my map look like? _____
_____
_____

INDUSTRY

Is this giving me a headache? _____
_____
_____

Is this something I can adjust?_____
_____
_____

If so, what does my map look like? _____
_____
_____

TRAVEL

Is this giving me a headache? _____
_____
_____

Is this something I can adjust?_____
_____
_____

If so, what does my map look like? _____
_____
_____

OTHER:

Is this giving me a headache? _____

_____

_____

Is this something I can adjust?_____

_____

_____

If so, what does my map look like? _____

_____

_____

OTHER:

Is this giving me a headache? _____

_____

_____

Is this something I can adjust?_____

_____

_____

If so, what does my map look like? _____

_____

_____

Worksheet #1:
Evaluation of the Now:
External Influences Summary

Once you have completed the worksheet, note the top three most frustrating items and your action steps to address them below so you can pay special attention to these areas as you proceed.

Most frustrating areas & action steps:

1. _____

Action steps: _____

_____

_____

2. _____

Action steps: _____

_____

_____

3. _____

Action steps: _____

_____

_____

CHAPTER 4

Internal Influences: What to Do about that Hole in Your Cheek

DAY 3

Do any of these statements sound like you?

- I stay awake at night thinking about how I could leave my job.
- I worry that I'm wasting time by not doing something more fulfilling, but I don't know what I could be doing instead.
- I feel like a robot at work, and I'm not sure if my brain even works anymore.
- I miss having the opportunity to share ideas and build something meaningful.
- I wonder if I could be doing more with my potential, creativity, and drive.

Feelings of worthlessness, invisibility, and dread are so common that we almost forget we don't have to accept them as a way of life. I once had a job that would make me feel sick every Sunday night. The longer I stayed at the job, the more of my weekend was consumed by dread. Most days, I would cry on my way to work and wonder if there was a semi-safe way to crash my car so I wouldn't have to go. One day, I actually did get a flat tire. I was overjoyed! Hanging out in a dirty garage for a few hours instead of going to work is one of my best memories of that job.

I've talked with hundreds of people who feel ignored, undervalued, and underpaid at work, but they stay. Why? For many, it's because they think they can't get anything better, and they don't want to risk losing what they have. They don't feel good, but the alternative could be worse, so they stay. The negative feelings they are experiencing about the lack of fulfillment is what I mean by "internal influences." While quitting your job is a complex decision, an important first step is to recognize that staying can be more harmful than trying something new.

In this chapter, we will explore your internal influences and how they are affecting you. Internal influences range from mental health and creative outlets to physical health and freedom to explore your imagination and ideas. Later, we will use the HAM Method from Chapter 3 to identify which of these areas are a headache, what you would like to adjust, and take the time to create your map.

~~~

Immersing yourself in your daily routine and task list is easy to do when you are trying to avoid that feeling of doom and gloom stemming from your job. However, what if you stopped and took an afternoon to evaluate what's bothering you, what's missing, and what you want most? Often, getting out of a bad situation starts with lifting your head up from the day-to-day and thinking about the future. Allow yourself some time to dream and reflect. Imagine your ideal life. What does it look like?

Thomas Robert Clarke of Titusville, New Jersey, did just that. As the regional sales representative for a boutique printing company, he started off as a happy employee who gradually grew unsatisfied with his work. Poor decisions made at the ownership level led to seasoned employees exiting the company, reduced product quality, and missed deadlines. Over time, as stresses increased, his healthy lifestyle decreased. Thomas says, "One morning I woke from a nightmare in which I saw myself ten years down the road after two divorces and as many heart attacks." This dream led to a 48-hour soul-searching session about the meaning of money and happiness. He asked himself, "What could I do with the rest of my life if money never came?" His answer kept coming back to photography and his next steps became obvious. Thomas is now owner of Thomas Robert Clarke Photography in New Jersey. While the road has been long and not always easy, once he committed 100 percent to his business, he immediately saw dividends. Thomas says, "In a few short years I went from having zero presence in a new city to being voted one of the Top 10 Best Photographers in the region."

If you're lucky, you get to experience a dream like Thomas' to get you thinking differently. That's not always the case. When Jake Van Loon of Wixom, Michigan, was informed of the untimely death of a close friend, he took this unfortunate accident as a sign. At that time, he was cooking at a popular local restaurant over fifty hours per week and, upon learning of his friend's death, fell into a depression that sparked a process of reevaluation. During his reflection period, he recognized he needed to give his dream of being a professional musician his full-time attention, and now. Jake left his job at the restaurant and is now the lead guitarist in Pulp Culture, an inspiring, uncompromising art rock band delivering performances for a good cause. He says, "I'm incredibly happy with my decision to throw myself fully into the music industry. Although each day brings its own beasts, I love meeting and learning from talented musicians, sound engineers, venue owners and booking agents who make live music possible every single night."

Life-changing events aren't always what we need in order to make a change, and that was the case with Trudy Scott of Folsom, California. When Trudy was in her late thirties, she was working in a high-stress, high-paying computer job. She suffered terribly from anxiety and unexplained fears. She often woke with a sense of doom. It got so bad, Trudy even had three panic attacks that included a racing heart, clammy skin, and hyperventilating. Literally, she thought she was going to die. Recognizing this was not normal, she decided to seek help from professionals; she saw a nurse practitioner and a naturopath to explore her options. She utilized natural solutions like gluten elimination and the healing power of nutrients like GABA, zinc, and B vitamins. By following their advice, she was able to eliminate the anxiety and panic attacks and once again lead a healthy life. Trudy says, "I actually then left my high-paying six-figure corporate job and went back to school to study nutrition. My dream was to start my own nutrition consulting business to help other women who experience this so they can feel on top of the world again." Trudy is now living her dream as a Food-Mood expert, nutritionist, and owner of The Antianxiety Food Solution. She educates women about real whole food and finding natural solutions for anxiety and stress, depression, and emotional eating problems. She even published a book, *The Antianxiety Food Solution* in 2011.

While many people can no doubt relate to Trudy's story, you may be saying to yourself your situation isn't *that* bad. Perhaps you're sitting at work doing a job that doesn't allow you to use your creative abilities and that one fact is enough to get you re-evaluating. Fortunately, your ideas and vision may make perfect sense if you took the time to explore them and present them to the right audience. Craig Wolfe of San Rafael, California, was excelling in his career but missing the fulfillment. He was the largest publisher of artwork from television commercials in the country for giants such as Coca-Cola, Anheuser-Busch, and M&M/Mars. Despite all of his success, he didn't enjoy working under other people's creative direction. He wanted to create his own unique whimsical brand, one that was closer to an expression of who he was. He decided to leave his job and started CelebriDucks, a company that creates celebrity rubber ducks of the greatest icons of film, music, history, and athletics. Craig says, "It sounded like a crazy idea, but I knew it would 'float.' " So far, they've sold over a million ducks, were voted one of the top 100 gifts by *Entertainment Weekly*, and have been featured on hundreds of media outlets including *The Tonight Show*.

Your crazy ideas may not have a place where you are today, but they may be exactly what you should be working on. Do you have a rubber ducky idea? Are you ready to "float" with it?

As in Chapter 3, we will use the HAM Method to evaluate the internal influences that are driving you to make a change. Take your time thinking about how important each of these elements are to you and if you are fulfilled in each area.

WORKSHEET #2:
INTERNAL INFLUENCES—
EVALUATION OF NOW

MEANINGFUL WORK
Is this giving me a headache? _____

_____

_____

Is this something I can adjust?_____

_____

_____

If so, what does my map look like? _____

_____

_____

CREATIVE FULFILLMENT
Is this giving me a headache? _____

_____

_____

Is this something I can adjust?_____

_____

_____

If so, what does my map look like? _____

_____

_____

APPRECIATION & RESPECT

Is this giving me a headache? _____

_____

_____

Is this something I can adjust?_____

_____

_____

If so, what does my map look like? _____

_____

_____

MENTAL STIMULATION

Is this giving me a headache? _____

_____

_____

Is this something I can adjust?_____

_____

_____

If so, what does my map look like? _____

_____

_____

PHYSICAL HEALTH

Is this giving me a headache? _____

_____

_____

Is this something I can adjust?_____

_____

_____

If so, what does my map look like? _____

_____

_____

ADVANCEMENT & GROWTH OPPORTUNITIES
Is this giving me a headache? _____

_____

_____

Is this something I can adjust?_____

_____

_____

If so, what does my map look like? _____

_____

_____

OTHER:
Is this giving me a headache? _____

_____

_____

Is this something I can adjust?_____

_____

_____

If so, what does my map look like? _____

_____

_____

Worksheet #2:
Internal Influences Summary

Once you have completed the worksheet, note the top three most frustrating items and your action steps to address them below so you can pay special attention to these areas as you proceed.

Most frustrating areas & action steps:

1. _____

Action steps: _____

_____

_____

2. _____

Action steps: _____

_____

_____

3. _____

Action steps: _____

_____

_____

Now that you've done the external and internal influences exercises, reflect on your current situation. Is this what you expected to see? Were there any surprises? What stands out to you? Pay special attention to the parts that really speak to you and feel especially gut-wrenching and note them below or in your Personal Escape Plan. These are the elements of your story you will want to hang onto as you go through the book.

Notes: _____

_____

_____

_____

_____

_____

_____

_____

_____

_____

_____

_____

_____

_____

_____

_____

_____

_____

_____

_____

_____

_____

_____

_____

_____

_____

_____

_____

_____

CHAPTER 5

Why Entrepreneurship?

DAY 5

At a party I recently attended, I met a guy named Brian who told me he stocked shelves for a living. He looked embarrassed as he told me this, and I asked why he was making that weird, I-think-I-just-ate-raw-chicken face. He said he hated his previous job but didn't know what he wanted to do next. Instead of making an impulsive move, he decided to get a simple job stocking shelves at a big box store overnight in order to have some downtime and think about what was important to him. Because Brian had a college degree and had been making a good salary, he felt like a loser every time someone asked him what he did for a living. I might be biased, but I told him I thought it was awesome that he was doing that for himself. Instead of giving in to the pressure to have a prestigious job in fear of what others would think, he was doing what he wanted and taking things slowly. He said his plan was to pay off his car and then go to school for Chinese Medicine so he could open his own acupuncture practice. In the meantime, he was enjoying the solitude of working at night, doing a simple job, and having little to worry about.

I mention this story because this chapter asks you to think about why you are considering entrepreneurship as a lifestyle and whether or not you are ready. You are probably arriving at the moment where you are asking yourself what it will really take to pull off a new business. This is normal. You might be saying, "Can I do this? Am I strong enough? Who the hell am I?" Good questions. If this is the case, you are going to love the rest of this chapter.

If you really, really, really hate your job and you're just looking for a way out, I want you to consider Brian's story. You may need an in-between job to hold you over until you can make better decisions. Sometimes when we are under stress and want to improve our situation, we make crazy decisions that seem totally logical. You've heard of the "rebound" after a bad breakup, right? Same idea. You just had your heart broken, you feel like a piece of poo freshly scraped off the bottom of a horseshoe, and you want to make yourself feel better. You look for a quick fix that will mend your heart and make you feel like yourself again. However, creating a rebound business to act as a bandage for a broken spirit is likely not the right motivation to create a lasting, sustainable livelihood. Knowing the difference between a longtime coming and an impulse decision will pay off in the long run.

Now is your chance to reflect and think about what's motivating your decision to start a business. Are you running *towards* something, or running *away* from something? You can do both, but recognize your true motivation now. This will be critical as you continue to decide whether or not starting a business is right for you.

Your motivation is:_____

_____

Why Start a Business?

A 2014 study conducted by Gallup[2] reported that more than eight in ten US small-business owners said they would start a business again if they had the choice. As cited in the study, reasons business owners are satisfied with self-employment are:

---

2 "Most US Small Business Owners Would Do It Again." *Gallop.* Newport, Frank, Web. May 20, 2014.

- More independence
- Job satisfaction and meaning
- Being their own boss/being the decision-maker
- Having a flexible schedule/more time with family
- Interacting directly with customers

These findings are consistent with the data I collected from every business owner I interviewed as well. In my survey, 100 percent of them indicated that they would, indeed, do it over again. The reasons?

Finding the right path:

Lisa Marie Latino of Long Shot Productions in East Hanover, New Jersey, says, "When I started my business, it was the first time in my life I felt that I was truly on the right path. The sleepless nights, the computer freak outs, the annoying customers and the periods of no social life were completely, totally worth it."

Creating freedom:

Chris Landry of Landry Communications in Northampton, Massachusetts, says, "I can't imagine working a real job ever again. I'm addicted to the freedom. Some people say that everyone should be self-employed, and I don't think that's true—it takes a high tolerance for risk, among other things—but I love the challenge and the rewards of what I'm doing."

Building mental strength & toughness:

Kristina Villarini of Villarini Maclean, a digital marketing business in New York City, says, "Business ownership made me smarter, stronger, and tougher. I'd do it all over again in a heartbeat—win, lose or draw. Don't regret, just rebuild."

Opportunities to learn and grow:

Nadine Sabulsky, aka The Naked Life Coach of Phoenix, Arizona, says, "Overall I'd say I'm extremely satisfied that I chose this path, and I expect it will keep motivating me to grow and learn beyond what I could have ever imagined when I started four years ago! And that, to me, is what is most important."

Life becomes an adventure:

Tammy Gunn of The Live Out Loud Movement in Toronto, Ontario, says, "The main reason I'm happy with this decision is that I see life as being too short to be stuck doing something I am really not lit up about just to guarantee a paycheck. I see life as a roller coaster and if it doesn't have its ups and downs, then it's more like flatlining and not really living at all. Adventures come when you step out of being comfortable. It's where living truly happens!"

Why Do You Want to Start A Business?

The reasons you want to start your business are completely unique and personal. That's why it is often hard to get good advice from others. When I announced to my family I was starting a business, I had an older family member try to talk me into getting a secure job with him because he was worried I would end up on the street and not be able to pay my bills. I felt like he wasn't listening to me and didn't believe that I could do it, which left me feeling deflated and insecure. As I thought about it more, he didn't realize that the risk was a big part of what was motivating me. It was an opportunity to prove myself and push myself more than I ever had before. I wasn't seeking security; I was seeking an adventure. If you seek out people with different values for advice, and you don't clearly define *why* you want to do what you want, you will receive a lot of unhelpful feedback. Before you start asking others for advice or validation, figure out for yourself what is motivating your decision and why it's important to you. In this chapter's worksheet, you'll get a chance to rate what is inspiring your thoughts about self-employment so you can identify what matters most.

WORKSHEET #3:
WHY ENTREPRENEURSHIP?
EVALUATION OF MOTIVATION

Step 1: Map out what you are hoping to achieve by starting a business. Take your time with this one! This is a great chance to grab a cup of coffee, your favorite pen, and a comfy chair so you can really think about what you want before you proceed through the book.

Directions: Next to each category, indicate its importance by picking a number between 1 and 3.

1 = very important

2 = somewhat important

3 = not at all important

I WANT:

_____ The freedom to be me

_____ To live my calling

_____ To have fun

_____ To pursue my ideas

_____ To work with a friend/business partner

_____ To get out of my current situation

_____ An adventure/change

_____ Financial independence

_____ To start over

_____ To prove something to myself and/or others

_____ To do meaningful, powerful work

_____ To stop living a lie

_____ To have control over my life

_____ To push myself

_____ Professional & personal development

_____ Job satisfaction

_____ To dedicate my life to a movement

_____ To wake up happy every day

_____ Location independence

_____ Other:
_____ Other:

Step 2

List the top 10 by importance, starting with those rated *very important*, continuing to *somewhat important* until you have filled every spot.

1. _____

2. _____

3. _____

4. _____

5. _____

6. _____

7. _____

8. _____

9. _____

10. _____

Step 3

Go through each box in the grid and circle the item that you would prioritize as more important to you today. For example, in the top box with the number 1 and the number 2, you are comparing items 1 and 2 in the list you just created. Which one is more important to you? Circle that one and continue until you have circled a number in each box.

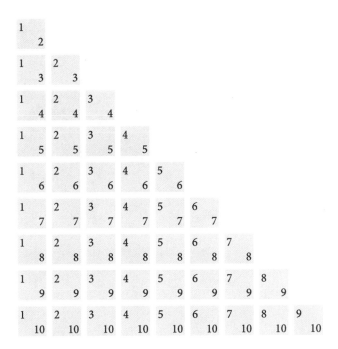

Step 4

How many times did you circle each item in your Top 10?

1	2	3	4	5	6	7	8	9	10

Step 5

Select the numbers with the highest values below them. Which items do these numbers correspond to from Step 2? List them below.

1. _____

2. _____

3. _____

You now have the three biggest motivators for starting a business! Do they look the way you thought they would? Keep these close. Right them on a giant poster board, note them on a Post-It and stick it on your bathroom mirror. You will want to be reminded of your motivation as you go through this book, and, if you decide you do want to start a business, you will want them front and center as you dig into building your new lifestyle.

CHAPTER 6

Your Lifestyle Designed

DAY 7

If you've been to church, attended a workshop aimed at professional growth, or have an interest in personal development, I have no doubt you've been asked to think about your values. You could easily come up with a long list of what you value ranging from your friends to a good meal, but those examples aren't the type of values we're addressing in this chapter. While a sunny day and a Hawaiian pizza are valuable, I want you to think about the values that lie at the heart of everything you do, otherwise known as your core values. Your core values are your compass: they point you in the direction you want to go. They are at the heart of your decisions and therefore need to be identified now, before we go deeper into this self-assessment. Without an awareness of your values, you will have a hard time deciding if business ownership is right for you and, if it is, building a business that meets your vision of success and works for the lifestyle you desire.

WORKSHEET #4:
YOUR CORE VALUES IDENTIFICATION[3]

Place a number ranging between 1 and 3 next to each value.
   1= very important
   2= somewhat important
   3= not important

_____ Caretaking (people, animals)
_____ Freedom (independence, free choice)
_____ Equality (fairness, equal opportunity to all)
_____ Self-respect (belief in oneself)
_____ Happiness (content, peacefulness)
_____ Wisdom (a mature understanding of life)
_____ Friendship (companionship)
_____ Accomplishment (achievement)
_____ Inner harmony (freedom from inner conflict)
_____ Comfort (prosperous, abundant)
_____ Mature love (sexual and spiritual intimacy)
_____ Beauty (nature and the arts)
_____ Pleasure (an enjoyable, leisurely life)
_____ Social recognition (respect, admiration)
_____ Exciting life (stimulating, active life)
_____ Ambition (hard working, aspiring)
_____ Openness (broadminded)
_____ Competence (effective)
_____ Cheerfulness (lighthearted, joyful)
_____ Cleanliness (neat, tidy)
_____ Courage (standing up for your beliefs)
_____ Forgiveness (willing to see past differences)
_____ Helpfulness (working for the betterment of others)
_____ Honesty (sincere, truthful)
_____ Imagination (daring, creative)

---

3 Values based upon work from Milton Rokeach

_____ Independence (self-reliant, self-sufficient)
_____ Intellect (intelligent, reflective)
_____ Logic (consistent, rational)
_____ Affection (tender)
_____ Obedience (dutiful, respectful)
_____ Courtesy (well-mannered)
_____ Responsibility (dependable, reliable)
_____ Self-control (restrained, self-disciplined)

List your top 10 values below starting with those rated *very important*:

1. _____

2. _____

3. _____

4. _____

5. _____

6. _____

7. _____

8. _____

9. _____

10. _____

Go back through your list of your top 10 and ask yourself, "Does this value guide me in all areas of my life, including work, relationships, personal choices, and interests?" Circle the values that result in a yes, and write your circled answers below.

Out of your circled answers, which are the three most important values that you feel clearly define you? List the three here:

1. _____

2. _____

3. _____

Are you surprised? The first time I did an exercise like this, I was shocked at how different my three core values were from what I assumed they were. I always thought my core values would be courage, ambition and freedom, but instead they are health, inner harmony, and self-respect. It is true that these three values are at the core of my thinking, even if I wasn't able to see that before.

What Does Success Look Like to You?

Refer to your newly identified core values as you define what success looks like. As you go through the book, you will notice I use the word "success" in an ambiguous way; it is thrown in to alert you that what you seek can be found by following the advice. Looking back at your core values, how does your success story play out? For example, if one of your core values is comfort, maybe your success story looks like you sitting on a beach somewhere wrapped in the world's softest towel and strumming a ukulele. Or, maybe one of your core values is power and your success looks like being the CEO of a 250-employee company. Whatever your core values are, use those to help you identify the lifestyle you want to create through your success:

Core Value #1:
What Success Looks Like: _____

Core Value #2:
What Success Looks Like: _____

Core Value #3:
What Success Looks Like: _____

Now that you have three pictures of success based on your core values, let's put them all together to design your ideal lifestyle. Here is an example:

Core value #1: Achievement

What success looks like: An award-winning business owner

Core value #2: Freedom

What success looks like: No set hours; single with limited personal commitments and location independence.

Core Value #3: Friendship

What success looks like: Continuously building meaningful friendships with ambitious, fabulous people all over the world.

Lifestyle design: A single entrepreneur with friends worldwide and a thriving business.

Write a sentence or two below that encapsulates your core values and visions of success. Lifestyle design is another way to define your vision of "perfect" and what you would like to happen if you do everything in a way that is right for you. **Your Ideal Lifestyle Design:**

_____

_____

_____

_____

_____

_____

CHAPTER 7

What Are You Really
Passionate About?

DAY 9

Guess the most popular question I am asked. No, it's not "Why are you so tall?"—although that comes up a lot (I'm six feet). The most popular question is: "How do I figure out what I'm passionate about?" This is the million-dollar question! There is actually a great way to figure this out and it costs you nothing. No personality assessment, and no silent retreat on a mountain needed. It's possible that you have a business idea but you're not sure if it's the right idea for you to run with because you're still not sure what you're passionate about. This chapter will address your passion and help you see if what you are thinking about matches with what you like doing.

Through years of observation, I've discovered the reason most people don't know what they are passionate about. Are you ready for this? It is because we overlook the mundane day-to-day tasks and don't realize we can label them as something we are "passionate" about. Instead, we think we are supposed to be focused on swimming with the dolphins, saving stray cats, working on a cure for cancer, or taking off to the moon. All of these endeavors are entirely possible paths for you, but we need to start a bit smaller in order to identify where your passions lie.

Let's start by making a list of micro-tasks to reveal bits of information to help you see you are likely already living your passion every day.

I'll give you an example from my life that has helped me immensely. I have always loved to cook and get so deep in the zone that I have to kick my husband out of the kitchen because I can't process a conversation. The fact that I love cooking so much would lead one to believe that it would make sense for me to be a chef or open a restaurant. When asked if I want to be a chef, the answer is no. I love to cook, but I don't want to do it for a living. Why? This list of micro-tasks and my evaluation of each one will help you see why I don't want to be a professional chef— that cooking is not actually what I am passionate about. You can use this example as a guide for this next exercise you will complete.

To start, I am going to break up all of the steps that go into cooking into micro-tasks and evaluate each one independently of the others. I am evaluating how each step makes me feel on a scale of 1 to 5. Here is how the scale works:

- 1 = unhappy
- 2 = somewhat unhappy
- 3 = neutral
- 4 = somewhat happy
- 5 = extremely, hop-out-of-my-socks happy

I also state *why* I gave it this score so I can put some thought into the micro-task, not the project as a whole. This is critical! To do this correctly, I have to realize I am no longer cooking a meal: I am going through a set of instructions to complete a project, like building a desk from IKEA, but way less annoying.

Micro-task #1: Recipe Search   Evaluation of task: 4

I want to make dinner tonight. What should I make? I search for recipes online for inspiration.

Why: I enjoy solving problems (what to cook?), I love looking at pictures of food, and I get excited about creating something.

Micro-task #2: Scheduling Evaluation of task: 4
Print out recipe and make a schedule for the afternoon. This includes when to go to the store, what I need to get, and when I will start cooking.

Why: I geek out on organizing my thoughts and creating efficiencies. Plus, planning out when I am going to the store and when I will start cooking eases concern over when I will fit this in with the work I need to get done before then.

Micro-task #3: Driving Evaluation of task: 3
Why: Driving is a necessary task, not one I look forward to or loathe.

Micro-task #4: Shopping Evaluation of task: 2
Why: Nothing new or exciting about it, just a necessary task. I don't like trying to get through crowded aisles, searching for items, and waiting in long lines.

Micro-task #5: Unpacking Groceries Evaluation of task: 2
Why: Mundane but necessary. There is nothing fun about putting the items in the cabinets and fridge.

Micro-task #6: Planning Evaluation of task: 5
Why: This is where I get super jazzed up and go into the zone. I love figuring out how to order the operations to maximize efficiency and have everything ready at the same time.

Micro-task #7: Cooking Evaluation of task: 5
Why: I go into a Zen-like meditation where I get extremely focused on the food and the process of slicing, stirring, and planning all while managing the clock. It is exhilarating, and I gain a sense of accomplishment as I look at each finished product.

Micro-task #8: Eating Evaluation of task: 4
Why? Believe it or not, my favorite part of cooking isn't actually eating! My food usually comes out tasting delicious, but it's the process of making it that gets me more excited.

Micro-task #9: Dishes   Evaluation of task: 1

Why? Let's just say I am eternally grateful for the invention of the dishwasher.

Although this exercise may seem long and tedious, it's helpful to break down your favorite activities into micro-tasks so you can evaluate *what* you really love about what you love. In this example, I learned that I love the following:

- Research (recipe search)
- Organizing my time and looking for efficiencies (planning afternoon, cooking)
- Creating and building (planning the order of operations, measuring, prepping ingredients)

If you look at those three activities independently of cooking, they boil down to research, planning, and building. When these pieces of the process are separated from food, you can see they can be applied to many more professions outside the kitchen.

Getting back to the million-dollar question, what am I passionate about? Well, I'm passionate about research, planning, and building. What careers or businesses could those skills be useful in?

- Project Manager
- Scientist
- Market Analyst
- Town Planner
- Realtor
- Engineer
- Lawyer
- Business Coach (!)

The list goes on and on. Once you isolate the things you enjoy from the specific activity, you will find that what you are passionate about is applicable to many careers or businesses you might not have previously considered. This opens the door to thinking bigger, discovering skills and interests you never knew you had, and imagining yourself in different roles or industries.

Now it's your turn to discover what you are passionate about. You can do this exercise a hundred times with various activities. Remember, this worksheet is available at www.domakebusiness.com/book and can be downloaded and saved to your computer by entering the password DoItAnyway. Here are some examples:

- Planning a family vacation
- Planting a garden
- Writing poetry
- Hiking a mountain
- Playing with your kids
- Painting a room
- Going out to eat
- Watching TV
- Shopping for new clothes
- Swimming
- Getting your hair done
- Playing golf
- Refurbishing old furniture
- Designing a logo
- Mowing the lawn
- Making coffee

The list is endless. If you don't know what you enjoy doing, just pick something you find yourself doing often so you can get used to the exercise. The process of discovering your passions is a commitment to creating a better life for yourself and it may take some time. Just enjoy it and don't get stressed out about "doing it right." Make a commitment to keep learning and paying attention. Knowing what you are passionate about will give you good insight into whether or not you would enjoy running your own business. You can start below with your first passion exercise.

WORKSHEET #5:
YOUR PASSION EXERCISE

Activity you are rating: _____

Date: _____

Step 1: Scale evaluation for each micro-task:
- 1 = unhappy
- 2 = somewhat unhappy
- 3 = neutral
- 4 = somewhat happy
- 5 = extremely, hop out of my socks happy

Micro-task #1: _____ **Evaluation:**____

Description:_____

_____

_____

Micro-task #2: _____ **Evaluation:**____

Description:_____

_____

_____

Micro-task #3: _____ **Evaluation:**____

Description:_____

_____

_____

Micro-task #4: _____ **Evaluation:**____

Description:_____

_____

_____

Micro-task #5: _____ **Evaluation:**_____

Description:_____

_____

_____

Micro-task #6: _____ **Evaluation:**_____

Description:_____

_____

_____

Micro-task #7: _____ **Evaluation:**_____

Description:_____

_____

_____

Micro-task #8: _____ **Evaluation:**_____

Description:_____

_____

_____

Micro-task #9: _____ **Evaluation:**_____

Description:_____

_____

_____

Micro-task #10: _____ **Evaluation:**_____

Description:_____

_____

_____

Step 2: What did you learn?

Major areas you love:

1. _____

2. _____

3. _____

4. _____

Taken out of context, what is at the heart of each of these interests?

1. _____

2. _____

3. _____

4. _____

How could these skills be translated into career choices/business possibilities? If you are having a hard time seeing how your interests/skills could be translated into a career, check out Rasmussen College's free Career Aptitude Test here: http://www.rasmussen.edu/resources/aptitude-test/

1. _____

2. _____

3. _____

4. _____

5. _____

6. _____

7. _____

8. _____

9. _____

10. _____

Pay attention as you go through the book to see if the interests you listed here are the same passions that go into running a business. It's not essential that they match up; that's where business partners, employees, and contractors come in. Don't get discouraged if your passions don't match perfectly—this is an area to pay attention to as we discuss the other elements you need to focus on in the chapters to come.

CHAPTER 8

Your Strengths
& Weaknesses

DAY 11

If anyone were to ask me the most important lesson I've learned from being a business owner, I would say that business has more to do with learning about yourself than about any industry, any customer segment, or any product. If you are unaware of how you work best, what you believe about yourself, where your strengths and weaknesses lie, and where you need help, your business will take a long time to get off the ground or, unfortunately, it will go nowhere.

When I started my business in 2009, I was convinced I could do everything. If I didn't want to do something, I told myself it *wasn't* because I wasn't good at it, it was because I didn't *like* it and therefore wasn't going to do it. For example, it took me a while to sit down and admit to myself that I sucked at dealing with money. It also took me a while to admit to myself that I am an idea person who likes to explore those ideas, not look at spreadsheets all day. Dealing with receipts, record keeping, and plotting out every move I was going to make sounded like torture times ten.

The problem with this haphazard approach is the unwanted stress that came from not knowing a critical part of running a business. Even though I didn't want to admit it, I constantly worried about money and whether or not I could make ends meet. Once I decided I could no longer go on this way and confessed I had a lot to learn (and then took the time to learn what I needed to know), my business started to take off. Everything started flowing smoothly because I got really honest about what was working and what wasn't. This was the beginning of the self-reflection and self-awareness I needed to keep building on what I had already created.

~~~

It's true: we're not good at everything, even if our moms told us that growing up. One of the hardest and best things you can do for yourself is be honest with yourself about what you are not good at. When I used to interview job candidates, asking about the interviewee's weaknesses was my favorite question. I felt it was the most telling about the person's character, self-awareness, and areas in need of improvement. Ninety-five percent of the time, I would not get a satisfying answer. Most people don't know how to answer the question because they are so focused on selling themselves that they are afraid to talk about personal development. That's a shame, because there is incredible opportunity for growth when you reveal your weaknesses. It's a part of being human, and once you stop beating yourself up for not being perfect, it can actually be a lot of fun.

Many entrepreneurs are proud of the fact that they do everything in their business and wear the title of CEO like a badge of honor. While they have surely earned this title, the problem with doing it all is, well, we can't do it all. We're not good at everything, even if we want to believe we will be if we try hard enough. Marc Renson of Ambition Bistro figured out that building his business meant admitting he couldn't do it all. "I've come to learn to *hire* my weaknesses and to *work* my strengths. I love being in the middle of restaurant chaos, that lunch rush mayhem of phones ringing, steaming milk for cappuccinos, take-out orders, server banter, food tickets piling up, the chemistry of a well-oiled, fine-tuned busy restaurant, and everybody falling into place and achieving that final goal. I'm not a pencil pusher." After trying to deal with accountants, lawyers, sales reps, and tax documents, Marc realized that just wasn't what he was meant to do. In order to build this business, he hired people to help with the areas he wasn't good at—and focused on what he loved doing. As a result, he was able to publish a book about his experiences, *Is The Coffee Fresh? Drama dysfunction and daily life at a downtown coffee house,* and create a nationally known celebrity hot spot restaurant.

Thomas Robert Clarke of Thomas Robert Clarke Photography echoes Marc's sentiments. He says, "A great lesson from my dad was not to get bogged down doing the things you aren't good at or don't want to do. Time's too precious; outsource that stuff and build the costs into your fees."

But what if you are just starting out and don't have the resources to hire someone? Well, that's when you seek out solutions to help you manage your weakness. When Jake Van Loon, guitarist in Pulp Culture, noticed he wasn't getting all his work done at the end of every day, he found tools to help him change. "In starting this business I realized I was constantly struggling with time management," says Jake. Due to his social media habits and poor organizational skills, he recognized that he needed to create a routine of partitioning out his days by the hour. He even downloaded a social media app called Facebook Limiter, which kicked him off all social media sites after 10 minutes of use. Once he had the right tools in place, he could complete his work with ease.

Our weaknesses don't go away because we have recognized them. They require care, attention, and a disciplined approach to managing them. Knowing that I am likely to avoid entering my income and expenses each week, I actually have a reoccurring appointment set in my calendar each Friday afternoon to look at my week and what I did in sales and how much money I spent. I also have a list of six questions at the bottom of each daily task list to force myself to address the financial aspects and growth of my business. Here is what it looks like:

End of the Day: Six Reflections

1. How much money did I make today?
2. Did I spend any money on my business today? If so, track.

3. Did I have business travel today? If so, track mileage.
4. What did I learn today?
5. What will I do better tomorrow?
6. What was the best part of my day?

I go through these questions for a few reasons:

- I remind myself that I am running a business, not spending time on a hobby.
- I need to be diligent about my expenses so I can track for taxes and cash flow.
- I am a student and I am always learning. Forcing myself to look at what I learned each day will tell me if I am living this mindset or not.
- I like to remind myself to have fun and enjoy what I'm doing, which can be hard if I have a particularly difficult day.

Knowing your weaknesses and creating tricks to manage them are key elements to building a successful business. As hard as this is, it's one of the most important things to do. The first solution you come up with to deal with your weaknesses will surely not be the last—but it is the process of discovery and figuring out what works best for you that will make you a great business person.

Getting Personal

As you're probably starting to notice, business ownership is a personal journey that is very different for everyone. Your personality and your experiences will determine what you need to focus on, change, work through, and build upon. No two stories are alike and that is why you need to know yourself and be totally honest with what you are bringing to the business. It's okay if you don't know anything more than your idea right now. If you're a cabinetmaker and you want to start a business, that's great! Now, you will need to recognize what you need to learn and whether or not you need to hire anyone to help you.

It's important to note that you shouldn't get down on yourself if you don't know a lot about business yet. Every single business owner I spoke with for this book (including myself and tons of my clients) had to overcome obstacles, put themselves in difficult situations, make uncomfortable decisions, raise their hand and say, "I don't know what I'm doing," and keep pushing forward. No one is born with all the business skills it takes to do this right. Know that it is a journey, and it is the commitment to that journey that will pay off in the end.

In the next worksheet, you will determine your awareness of your strengths and weaknesses and how this knowledge can help you. This is another big exercise that may require more time to complete than you think. Sugarcoating your responses or flying through the exercise will make the rest of the journey more difficult, so don't be afraid to go deep and dark! (Don't worry, no one will be reading this but you.)

WORKSHEET #6:
WHAT DO YOU KNOW ABOUT YOURSELF?

Step 1: Directions: Circle the words that best describe you below, for better or for worse. Don't spend too much time thinking about each one. Go with your gut instinct.

Forceful	Passive	Indifferent	Arrogant
Fearful	Considerate	Friendly	Accurate
Enthusiastic	Aggressive	Intolerant	Lazy
Obstructive	Self-assured	Determined	Independent
Spontaneous	Bossy	Wasteful	Selfish
Pushy	Inspiring	Patient	Intelligent
Trustworthy	Chaotic	Stubborn	Complaining
Loose-tongued	Adventurous	Orderly	Tactful
Respectful	Cynical	Reckless	Impatient
Mistrustful	Lively	Disciplined	Creative
Tolerant	Blunt	Inhibited	Honest
Undisciplined	Persuasive	Ambitious	Shallow
Observant	Stand-offish	Naive	Straightforward
Sloppy	Serious	Dedicated	Strict
Optimistic	Vague	Greedy	Appreciative
Rude	Idealistic	Flexible	Shy
Caring	Inflexible	Fanatical	Versatile
Generous	Warm	Logical	Prejudiced
Short-sighted	Moody	Dull	
Practical	Humorous	Open	

Step 2:

Review your list and think about which personality traits are your strengths and which traits get in your way. List them in the corresponding column.

STRENGTHS: WEAKNESSES:

_____   _____
_____   _____
_____   _____
_____   _____
_____   _____

Step 3: How Your Strengths Can Help You

Your strengths listed in Step 2 could help you with the following business activities. Circle the activities you feel you will excel at based on your strengths.

- Dealing with customers
- Managing your time each day
- Managing your money
- Being disciplined and focused
- Setting long-term goals
- Selling yourself
- Coming up with creative marketing ideas
- Following through on promises
- Managing employees
- Researching business information
- Organizing data and records

Step 4: How Your Weaknesses Can Hold You Back

Your weaknesses listed in Step 2 could create challenges with the following business activities. Circle the ones you are concerned about.

- Dealing with customers
- Managing your time each day
- Managing your money
- Being disciplined and focused
- Setting long-term goals
- Selling yourself
- Coming up with creative marketing ideas
- Following through on promises
- Managing employees
- Researching business information
- Organizing data and records

Step 5: Addressing Your Weaknesses

Now that you know how your weaknesses will play out in business, what are some steps you could take for each weakness in an effort to address them, work through them, and manage them? These are steps you could take regardless of starting a business, as personal weaknesses can also be a hindrance when you are an employee or in other areas of your life. In other words, don't wait for the day you start a business to begin addressing areas of your life that you know are holding you back.

What can you do to manage or improve these weaknesses?

Weakness #1: _____

Plan to address it: _____

Weakness #2: _____

Plan to address it: _____

Weakness #3: _____

Plan to address it: _____

Weakness #4: _____

Plan to address it: _____

Keep track of these weaknesses in your Personal Escape Plan (along with the findings of the other five exercises you have completed). Creating a plan to work on them will start you off in a better place than if you ignore them and simply hope for the best. Remember, "ignorance is bliss" may be great in some settings, but when it comes to starting a business, the more information you have, the greater your chance of success.

A great resource for understanding your strengths and how to utilize them in your professional endeavors is *StrengthsFinder 2.0* by Tom Rath. It's a short online assessment (around fifteen minutes) that shows you your top five strengths and how they can be helpful to you in your career. I took the assessment six years ago and still refer to the book. It would be a great tool to go along with this exercise and can be found in my book list at www.domakebusiness.com/book.

CHAPTER 9

Your Beliefs

DAY 13

Do any of these statements sound like you?

- I could never do (insert scary thing here).
- I'm not the kind of person who takes risks.
- I wasn't born with the right talents/skills to run a business.
- I'm not old enough/smart enough/young enough/bold enough to try _____.
- I'm not a creative person.

What do all of these statements have in common? They are all beliefs, not facts. Merriam-Webster dictionary defines a belief as "a feeling of being sure that someone or something exists or that something is true." As you can see, beliefs are feelings, not facts. Yet, when we say these statements to ourselves, we believe them and take them for truth. This is where we get into trouble.

Besides learning important business skills, recognizing your strengths and weaknesses, finding your passions and identifying your value system, there is another important element of building a successful business: your belief system. You've no doubt heard advice given by famous and beloved icons who state the importance of belief. Sugar Ray Robinson, one of the greatest boxers ever to live said, "To be a champ, you have to believe in yourself when nobody else will." Harry Potter, the adored magician, reminds us that "Working hard is important. But there is something that matters even more: believing in yourself." Venus Williams, the four-time Olympic gold medalist tennis player, says, "Just believe in yourself. Even if you don't, pretend that you do and, and at some point, you will."

What this means is, if you believe you are destined to work in a crappy job forever and barely scrape by, you will probably work in a crappy job forever and barely scrape by (barring winning the lottery). If you believe you are the type of person who can build a business, be okay with failing occasionally and learn the skills necessary to keep growing, then you are starting with the right mindset. Your thoughts really do dictate your outcomes. It is the belief that we can do something that gets us started and keeps us going.

Another one of the most popular questions I am asked is, "How do you deal with the nagging internal voice that says, you're going to fail. You can't do this. Who do you think you are?" There are probably thousands of ways to address this (many of which I have tried), but I have found one in particular works very well. It's simple and the only catch is that you have to actually *do* it! This is not something you do once and you are fixed forever. This is a constant practice that will, over time, take hold and change what you believe about yourself. If you've ever been plagued by negative or limiting beliefs, you're going to love this.

1. Notice. Before any changes can occur, you have to notice something is happening. That means you have to catch your inner gremlin voice saying things like, "You're not creative" or "You're stupid for thinking this could work." Whenever you hear these beliefs, that's your clue it's time to pay attention.
2. Recognize. Now, you need to think about where that voice is coming from, because it's not yours. Did someone tell you this before? Did you hear it from a friend, family member, teacher, boss, or

somewhere else? Realizing that these voices are not part of you will help you separate from them.

3. Reframe. Since you caught the gremlin, you can now tell yourself the truth about yourself. Instead of believing that you're not creative, you can instead say to yourself (out loud or in your head), "I am a creative person with my own personal style and I have great ideas!" This reframing of your thoughts should give you the ability to keep going and move out of the negativity.

4. Repeat. Every time you hear negativity or limiting beliefs, that is your cue to notice, recognize, and reframe. Doing this over and over again will train you to quickly move through moments of debilitating thoughts and get you back on track.

Of course, there are many other ways to deal with beliefs besides this exercise, but this is a good place to start. One of my favorite authors, SARK, has written several books about self-awareness, beliefs, and how to do things you think are outside your reach. One of my favorites is *Prosperity Pie: How to Relax About Money and Everything Else.* This book is especially helpful if you want to look at your beliefs around money, success and abundance in your life. This book is available at www.domakebusiness.com/book along with every other recommended resource in this book.

As you start to look at your beliefs and separate them from your other thoughts, you may notice that many of your beliefs are old and deeply engrained. Perhaps they come from a parent, teacher or guidance counselor you trusted and believed had your best interests at heart. When you start to recognize that the stories you were told are just that—stories—you will realize that it is within your control to rewrite that story and make it your own. Such is the case with Michelle Dale, owner of VirtualMissFriday. com, a virtual assistant service based on the Island of Crete, Greece. Michelle says, "I was told by my career office when I left school at sixteen I would amount to nothing, that I would never earn more than a basic wage if I didn't have qualifications, and I should find a stable job with a pension plan and 'work my way up the ladder.' " Instead of following that advice, at the age of twenty-three, she took a bold move and quit her job. She left the country and started her own business. What did she learn by defying the advice given to her in her teenage years? "The biggest lesson I have learned, among many, is that it's not what you know that creates wealth and success in your life. It's what you believe is possible."

The power of belief is so strong that it is actually being studied by leading scientists and medical researchers. Bruce Lipton, PhD, is an internationally recognized leader in the field of new biology. His book, *The Biology of Belief*, uncovers new science showing that genes and DNA do not control our biology; instead, DNA is controlled by signals from outside the cell, including the energetic messages emanating from our thoughts. This groundbreaking work tells us that we are in control of changing our lives through the power of thought—rather than being dealt a hand we have no control over. While this research is in the early stages, it is the beginning of understanding that what we tell ourselves makes a big impact on who we are and what we believe we are capable of. If you catch yourself saying, "I can't do that," this may be your cue to start changing your thoughts so you can change your life.

Next, you will take a look at your current beliefs about yourself. You will get to see for yourself, on paper, which beliefs may be holding you back from taking steps towards business ownership. Be careful not to judge yourself or censor your thoughts—this is an exercise to get everything out, not worry about what sounds right.

WORKSHEET #7:
YOUR BELIEFS

Step 1: Set a timer for five minutes. Now, use the white space below to write in all of the beliefs you have about yourself. This list should contain the good, the bad, and the ugly. For example, your list could contain items like "I am pretty," "I am destined to be unhappy," or "I make terrible decisions." Don't worry about whether or not these beliefs are pure fiction or the truth—just write.

_____

_____

_____

_____

_____

_____

_____

Step 2: Look back through the list of beliefs you wrote and ask yourself the same question for each: "Is this true?" Statements that are FACTS are true. Statements that are BELIEFS are usually false.

TRUE   FALSE

_____   _____

_____   _____

_____   _____

_____   _____

_____   _____

Step 3: For all of the beliefs in the FALSE column, use the four-step exercise to analyze where it came from and how you can reframe it.

- Notice: Catch yourself caught in a limiting belief.
- Recognize: Consider where this belief came from, why you are carrying it around with you.
- Reframe: Twist the belief so it is true and representative of who you really are.
- Repeat: Practice this exercise every time you are thinking negative/limiting beliefs.

As you go through each false belief, rewrite the true version in the TRUE column, and put a line through the old version of the belief. When you're done, you should have a lengthy list of truths about who you really are, not who you've been telling yourself you are.

Step 4: List your most surprising truths below. What stands out to you as different from what you have been telling yourself?

1. _____

2. _____

3. _____

CHAPTER 10

How's Your Sales Face?

DAY 15

In addition to the many benefits of self-employment, there is a good deal of work involved in just letting people know your business exists. In an April 2014 Gallup poll[4] of small business owners, some of the biggest challenges they uncovered were building a customer base, generating revenue, and selling. These topics have their own chapter because they amount to roughly *half* of what you spend time on in your business for at least the first few years.

Building Your Customer Base

Many business owners excel at their craft, but lack the business skills to get the word out about what they are doing and why customers should pay for it. Sales is one the two main areas where the job is never done, marketing being the other. There is always more to learn about conveying

---

4 "Most US Small Business Owners Would Do It Again." *Gallop*. Newport, Frank, Web: http://www.gallup.com/poll/169592/small-business-owners-again.aspx. May 20, 2014.

a message, reaching a market, packaging your product or service, and serving your customer.

While making barstools and websites are fun activities, the *business part* of the business doesn't actually start until people are aware of what you are doing, you are getting your products in the hands of strangers, and you are doing this for a price. Without these critical steps, you have a hobby, not a business. One person who turned her hobby into a business is Brigit Esselmont of Balaclava, Australia. Her love of reading Tarot cards turned into a business idea when she noticed people were willing to pay for her readings. As she started to explore how feasible her idea was she quickly learned that reading Tarot is really only half of what needs to be done; the other half is knowing how to market yourself and sell your offerings. Brigit says, "When I started to get serious about growing my business, I realized I needed to master the art of authentic sales and marketing. I invested in learning how to write compelling copy, use email marketing to build relationships, create high-impact Facebook ads, and create offerings that I knew my community would love and value. Now, authentic sales and marketing is one of the most engaging aspects of my work—I love it!" Brigit is owner of BiddyTarot. com, a website that inspires over a million people each year to transform their own lives and others' with the Tarot.

Like Brigit, Lisa Hennessy of Chicago, Illinois, quickly learned the importance of crafting compelling sales techniques. As the owner of Your Pet Chef, a raw diet for pets, she sees sales and marketing as an evolving process and builds her strategy around what her customers are telling her. "I've learned to be adaptable with my message. I perfected my pitch at trade shows after getting hundreds of what I call "the face"—a scrunched-up nose and a puzzled look. When I said I make raw food for dogs, I realized that people thought I had raw organ meat in a bag. I now say I make personalized dog food, and I reach down into my cooler and show them the food while saying, "it's a raw diet." I rarely see "the face" anymore!"

Generating Revenue

It's important to add that the end goal in all this sales and marketing talk is to generate revenue to keep your business alive. While this may seem obvious, it's the money part of selling that gets some business owners tripped up. The concern over making the sale can be so overwhelming that the learned techniques or slick website don't matter because the business owner is tripping over themselves while trying to close a deal. When Lisa Marie Latino, owner of Long Shot Productions in East Hanover, New Jersey, recognized that talking about money was the hardest part of selling, she dealt with it head-on. She enrolled in sales classes to broaden her understanding of the art and learn tips to calm her nerves. Due to her new skills, she no longer undersells her product. Lisa says, "Having a fear that's holding you back can be detrimental to the health and longevity of your business. It's important to recognize your drawbacks, improve upon them, and keep growing and learning."

Conversely, you could be a great people person and enthusiastically talk about your products with prospects all day while also lacking the follow-through it requires to close a deal. Since the sales process is often lengthy and may require several presentations, it's easy for a business owner to get distracted and miss out on a sale because they are focused on other elements of the business. "I'm a natural networker and connector with strong relationship building skills. I'm even disciplined enough to make the first follow-up contact, but then I'm onto the next thing and the lead dies," says Elene Cafasso, owner of Enerpace, Inc., an executive coaching firm in Elmhurst, Illinois. When she learned where she dropped the ball in the sales process, she decided to work around her weakness. She hired a virtual assistant and started using a customer relationship management (CRM) system. She trained her assistant to do the follow-up and keep in touch with prospects until they got an appointment or closed out the account. This small change in her sales process resulted in a big difference in her bottom line.

I can't say enough how important it is to recognize that once you step away from the security of a paycheck and decide to run your own business, it is up to YOU to generate revenue so you can pay yourself. Take a moment to visualize yourself talking to prospects, expressing what you do, and asking for money. How does that make you feel? It gets easier as you go, but you need to first be honest with yourself about whether or not this is something you can, and want, to do. Of course, you can learn sales skills and improve your approach, but if you're unwilling to try, your business will go nowhere without customers to support it.

WORKSHEET #8:
SKILLS TO LEARN

Go through each category and evaluate what you need to learn and what you already know. Don't worry if you don't know everything! This is an opportunity to create a starting point so you know what is needed.

1 = expert

2 = knowledgeable, but could learn more

3 = amateur/what the heck does that mean?

SALES SKILLS

_____ New business development

_____ Customer relationships

_____ Dealing with competition

_____ Talking about money

_____ Networking

_____ Copywriting

_____ Product knowledge

_____ Customer knowledge

_____ Industry trends

_____ Customer relationship management software

_____ Follow-up

_____ Closing deals

Worksheet #8:
Sales Skills to Learn Summary

Once you've completed the worksheet, note the top three items you need to learn and possible action steps to address them so you can pay special attention to these areas as you proceed.

Sales skills to learn:

1. _____

Action steps: _____

_____

_____

2. _____

Action steps: _____

_____

_____

3. _____

Action steps: _____

_____

_____

CHAPTER 11

A Simple Quiz About Work

DAY 17

An obvious, and key part of owning your own business is making sure the work gets done, whether it's by you, your business partner, or your team. When you are in charge, you no longer have a boss looming over you expecting your TPS Report by noon. There are no performance reviews (unless you want to impose that on yourself) and there is no negative reinforcement if you don't get your work done (except, maybe not making money or angering your clients). When it comes down to it, you are free to work when you want, where you want, and as much as you want. With this type of freedom, business owners can have a hard time creating structure, building discipline, and staying focused on their priorities.

The unfortunate thing about freedom is that everything feels loose and easily moveable—which can get business owners in trouble because there are no parameters to operate in. I find I get way more done when I create a schedule for myself and stick to it. If I don't have a plan to work from each morning, I can kiss half my day goodbye! I can easily spend way too much time checking email, reading the news, responding to Facebook posts, and organizing my office. Before I know it, it's time for lunch and nothing concrete has happened.

In order to set yourself up for success, it's best to recognize your habits, worth ethic, and awareness of whether or not you're the type of person who can work independently. It's easy to say you could do it, but do your past actions reveal that you are someone who is focused, disciplined and committed enough to get the job done without supervision or the fear of losing your job? This is an important part of recognizing whether or not business ownership is for you because at the heart of your business, is you, the engine, the self-propelled machinery that will make everything move forward. Without the ability to do so, your business will go nowhere fast.

Take this simple quiz about your work style and see what it reveals about you. Of course, past behaviors don't always indicate future outcomes, but they are a good test to show you what you would need to think about if you wanted to get a new business endeavor off the ground. Once you have answered the questions, see what the quiz reveals about you.

WORKSHEET #9:
A SIMPLE QUIZ ABOUT WORK

Self-Awareness: This is the foundation of your work habits. If you don't know where your weaknesses lie, it will be difficult to help yourself create systems and tricks to stay on top of your work when you would rather be at a bar with friends or watching a Family Guy marathon.

1. Are you aware of any counter-productive work habits, weaknesses, or limiting thoughts that prevent you from moving forward?
    _____ YES _____ NO

2. Have bosses/co-workers/clients shared constructive observations about your work habits that you agreed with and were willing to change?
    _____ YES _____ NO

3. Do you recognize when you are having self-destructive, limiting thoughts and if so, do you reverse them so you can push through them?
    _____ YES _____ NO

Personal Growth: Building a business means finding efficiencies, growing your skills, looking for work to delegate, and improving your stamina. If you are unwilling to invest in personal growth, you will find that your business will also have a hard time growing. Lifelong learners do best in self-employment because they are constantly able to tweak their systems and increase output. The idea is not to work more as your business grows, but to improve the way you work so you can get more from less.

4. Do you seek out opportunities to build your skill set, learn new tools, and increase your knowledge?
    _____ YES _____ NO

5. Do you think of life as an ongoing experiment by trying new things, learning from your mistakes, dreaming up new ideas and repeating the process?
    _____ YES _____ NO

6. Do you often read how-to, self-help, business, and other informational books in order to increase your awareness, understanding, and abilities?

_____ YES _____ NO

Discipline: This is the make or break skill that many business owners fail to master. Self-discipline requires extreme integrity and focus on your goals. If you lack discipline, it's easy to stall out and ruin a perfectly good business idea early on. I will say this again: the key to building a business is doing the work. Doing the work means putting your head down, working on your key goals, and consistently delivering a finished product. Without this, your business is doomed.

7. Do you finish projects you start if no one is there to hold you accountable?

_____ YES _____ NO

8. Do you have systems in place to ensure you get your work done by your deadline?

_____ YES _____ NO

9. If you make a list of priorities, do you work on those and make sure you don't drift into other projects?

_____ YES _____ NO

10. Can you stop yourself from doing easy work so you can do the important work?

_____ YES _____ NO

11. Do you look for new systems and solutions when you are unsure of what to do next, the work gets difficult, or you get scared?

_____ YES _____ NO

12. Do you catch yourself complaining and blaming others when things don't go your way, and instead take responsibility and work on your challenges until you've figured them out?

_____ YES _____ NO

13. Do you find pleasure in completing what you set out to do and see hard work as the key to success?

_____ YES _____ NO

Focus: While focus sounds like discipline, it's actually a bit different. Focus is the ability to pick your two or three major priorities and work on them until they are completed. When you are in business for yourself, it's easy to dream up new products, new services, and new marketing ideas and want to start working on them right away. Having new ideas is great – in fact, it's a big part of what will keep your business exciting and growing – but they can also hold you back if you start too many things at once and never finish anything. Focusing on your goals is a needed skill if you want to create a growth-oriented enterprise.

14. Are you able to pick a few major priorities and work on those, or are you constantly looking for new activities to keep your work exciting and fresh?

       _____ YES _____ NO

15. Do you have systems or a reward method in place so you are not easily distracted by impulse creating and lose interest in your goals?

       _____ YES _____ NO

16. Do you recognize that focusing on a few things at once is not a punishment, but one of the major keys to business success?

    ___ YES   _____ NO

Structure: Freedom is an amazing gift business owners are given when they choose this lifestyle. However, this freedom can be overwhelming to manage since each day is completely open for you to create. Without building a work structure to contain your work priorities, personal life, and activities like sleep and exercise, it's easy to let your entire life be consumed by work or be consumed by thinking about and worrying about work but getting nothing done.

17. Can you make a schedule and stick to it?

       _____ YES _____ NO

18. Do you have a set of goals you adhere to and methodically work through until they are done?

       _____ YES _____ NO

19. If no one was there to tell you how to do something, would you be able to create a plan for yourself to follow?

    _____ YES _____ NO

Commitment: This attribute is strongly aligned with focus, but it is not the same thing. While focus will allow you to work on the projects that matter, it's your commitment that will drive you to make sure they are done on-time and done well. If you are an impulse idea person and find that you can easily hop from a dog walking business to house painting in the course of one day, you may need to focus on commitment. Commitment can be honed and it comes back to your motivation, which we covered in chapter 5.

20. Would people describe you as someone who is committed to their dreams and doesn't stop until you have what you want?

    _____ YES _____ NO

21. Would you consider yourself someone who isn't afraid of where you are going and therefore doesn't find it difficult to lock yourself into one path or another?

    _____ YES _____ NO

22. Are you ready to commit to your dream and do whatever it takes to get there, comfortable or not?

    _____ YES _____ NO

That concludes our quiz! Now, count up your YES responses and list them here:?

    _____ YES

17-22 YES Responses:
Congratulations! You are a master worker who has already recognized the importance of building systems, focusing on your priorities, and building structure into your work day. While you may have a few key areas to improve, you are definitely someone who can work independently and keep the engine running while also driving the car. Make a note of the areas you could still improve and make a plan to address them before you start your business.

Areas to focus on:

_____

_____

_____

_____

_____

_____

11-16 YES Responses:

You are someone who does great work and does it on time, but may need the extra push or motivation from a team, a boss, or department metrics. While you are an excellent employee and have a superb track record, you may not be ready to work independently just yet. Look back at the quiz and notice which areas you indicated the most NO responses. These areas will need to be focused on and built up before you can work on your own. Of course, you can always take the chance and go for it now, but not having a larger chunk of the critical work habits in place when you start may slow you down and make each day a bit more difficult to get through. Note which areas you need to focus on and seek out resources to help you as soon as possible.

Areas to focus on:

_____

_____

_____

_____

_____

_____

1-10 YES Responses:

If you scored a low number of YES responses, you probably already know that the road of business ownership will be a tough one for you at this time. It's likely you are more comfortable being given work to complete than working on the big picture. This is helpful information for you because it lets you know what type of work is best for your personality and work style. Of course, skills can be learned and honed, and business ownership should not be ruled out, but know that you will have to commit to building those skills and creating an entirely new approach to your work. If you are ready for that challenge, start there and then reconsider business ownership in a year or two when you have these habits in place. Note which areas you'd like to focus on first and list them below. Get started by working on them one at a time or by building a system that helps you learn efficiently.

Areas to focus on:

_____

_____

_____

_____

_____

_____

CHAPTER 12

Self-Assessment Results

DAY 19

Let's take a moment to talk about how awesome you are, shall we?

You've already considered what's going on in your world right now and what it is that's bothering you. You've decided against wanting to pop your boss's tires because you now know there is a better way to seek revenge. You've evaluated your strengths, weaknesses, values, passions, and (hopefully) realized you are not as crazy as you thought.

I hope you had a celebratory sundae or giant plate of nachos to say, "Hey, I'm pretty cool!" What you have done so far is what so many people never get to because they stop themselves before this point. They believe they aren't cut out for business, they wouldn't be good at it, and it's too risky. So, hey, I'm happy for you. You already clobbered that mother beast and you're going for it. You should be happy for you, too, because you're killing it!

This chapter is dedicated to your personal inventory, your journey, and recognizing just how far you have come in a very short amount of time. There will be some writing involved, so I hope you have your pencil handy. Why? Because writing helps solidify thoughts. Just rolling them around in your head all day doesn't do much for action. The simple act of writing your ideas on paper helps them become clearer. Now you can see them! They are alive!

WORKSHEET #10:
PERSONAL INVENTORY

Step 1: How You're Feeling Today
Circle your reactions to what we've covered so far and write in your own.

Wow, I know more than I thought.   I want to go to sleep now.

This is a dream come true!   How am I going to pull this off?

I can't wait to get started!   What am I THINKING?

This isn't going to work.   I was MADE for this!

Step 2: Why You're Awesome
Next, list what you've learned about yourself so far and why you are awesome. Yes, really. I know from personal experience that it's easy to feel trapped between Camp Dread and Terrorville focusing only on your shortcomings and insecurities, so doing an exercise where you actually acknowledge that you've learned some things about yourself is incredibly satisfying. You may be tempted to jump past this exercise. Don't do it! Acknowledging how far you've come is just as important as recognizing what you need to learn. Now, grab your pencil. And yes, you will need to come up with at least ten things. Go!

What I've Learned About Myself:

1. _____

_____

2. _____

_____

3. _____

_____

4. _____

_____

5. _____

_____

6. _____

_____

7. _____

_____

8. _____

_____

9. _____

_____

10. _____

_____

Step 3: What I Want to Work On

We know you're amazing. But no human being is perfect, so what do you need to work on? Going back to the past exercises, what should you be focusing on? List at least five things below.

1. _____

_____

2. _____

_____

3. _____

_____

4. _____

_____

5. _____

_____

Step 4: Remaining Questions

Now, take an inventory of all your questions that still remain unanswered. What are you wondering about that hasn't been covered so far? Writing these questions down will demonstrate what you need to focus on as you continue this journey. If you can't think of any questions that apply to the work we just did, think about your business idea and what areas you are still unsure about. Go nuts writing all your questions down so you can free up some brain space for your big decision..

Questions:

1. _____

_____

2. _____

_____

3. _____

_____

4. _____

_____

5. _____

_____

6. _____

_____

7. _____

_____

8. _____

_____

9. _____

_____

10. _____

_____

Step 5: Should You Start a Business?

We've arrived at the big moment. The moment when we address the one question this entire book is attempting to answer. After all of the self-reflection and analysis you've done in the last eleven chapters, did you come to a conclusion? You don't need to know for sure yet if your business idea is feasible, but you should have an idea of where you stand on the topic of entrepreneurship. So, ask yourself the following question and circle your answer below.

Should I start a business?

YES   NO

**If you chose yes, you will love the rest of this book.
Keep going!**

**If you chose no, congratulations on ruling this
option out so you can focus on a new career path.
Next, read my first book, *The Anti-Résumé Revolution*,
to start creating your new plan.**

Step 6: Free Writing

Lastly, write down anything else on your mind, like the reason for your decision on whether or not to start a business. The intention is to address the questions still rolling around in the corners of your noggin and smash them into dust so you can actually sleep tonight.

Your Free Writing Area:

_____

_____

_____

_____

_____

_____

CHAPTER 13

If You Chose Yes

DAY 21

If you're still reading this, I assume it's because when you asked your-self the question, "Should I start a business?" you chose "yes." I'm also assuming that at this exact moment, you are sitting with a fire in your belly waiting to finish reading these words so you can finally start working on your new business and life.

If I just described you, the impatient creator, you are one of us. You are part of our family, and you can't imagine following the rules for one more minute and being told to wait to try that thing you have been craving all your life. You are ready to stop holding on for your turn.

You are joining the ranks of millions before you who also said, "It's time." You are lucky. You have found a path. A path that now you know *is* the one for you, and you can pour yourself into it wholeheartedly. When your mind, body, and soul are aligned, that is when the real magic happens.

My goal in writing this book was to move you from the dreaming stage to the doing stage. My motivation is, and always has been, to get people to stop waiting and start creating. Why? My absolute biggest fear is waking up one day in my 80s, looking back on my life, and being utterly disappointed because I didn't take any risks and go for it 100 percent. Wasting this precious life by wondering what "could be" is a terrifying thought. These thoughts remind me that I cannot, and will not, give up. Part of me not giving up is being a leader for others who want to live that same mantra.

What business ownership means to me is having an open road to creative expression and a lifestyle I get to build every day. It's a means to create real change using my, and only my, gifts and vision. I now feel, through a lot of trial and error, that at the bottom of my soul, I am doing the job I was put here to do. Some days, I'm scared to death. Other days, I am completely in my flow and hours pass like seconds. Having a life with this much variation and extremes is part of the adventure I love so much. You never know what the next day will bring; you get to create it.

It took me a long time—20 years—to finally circle back to who I really am and recognize my gifts as the tools I use in my business every day to inspire others. I learned this when I finally stopped rejecting who I thought I was "supposed to be" and let who I really am shine through. Now, I get to make videos every day, just like the ones I used to make when I was ten, eleven, and twelve years old. I get to make gifts and cards for the members of my community, the Do+Make Business District, just like the ones I've been making for friends and family my whole life. I've always loved to write and now I get to compose books, create presentations, and build classes where I share stories from my own life and show others that I, too, am on the same journey. Now that I am finally embracing the pieces of myself that have always been there, I am able to build a business that not only sustains me, but also fulfills me. I can't ask for anything more.

If you had the curiosity to pick up this book, read all the chapters, and arrive at this point, I hope you will take one final challenge before you go:

Make decisions from your heart and from your instincts. Don't deny the things you want most. Experiment. Try aiming to fail in the beginning and learn from those mistakes. Keep building. When you think you are not ready, that is the perfect time to start. The perfect day does not come unless you create it.

It's your turn to live the life you've been dreaming of. You will now become a role model for those around you. Step into your position as an uncompromising visionary and proceed fearlessly. This is your moment.

Your challenge is to choose today to start over. Mark today as Day 1 on your calendar, take a photo of yourself expressing this, and get to work.

Stop waiting for your journey to begin and start creating it. Your whole life is before you.

What's Next

This book, *Who's With Us?,* is book 1 of a two-part series. Part two, *Do+Make: The Handbook for Starting Your Very Own Business*, is where you learn how to assemble your dreams into a business that will support you. Now that we've covered a lot of personal reflection and understanding the type of lifestyle you want, in book 2, you get to dig into each piece of starting a business while also learning how to master the entrepreneurial mindset. Here is an overview of the topics we will cover in the same style (information and worksheets) in book 2:

- How to determine the best business type for you
- How to talk to your customers and figure out what they want
- How to set a start date and what to do to prepare
- How to build a team and who you should have help you
- How to create the heart and soul of your business
- How to put together a solid marketing plan and brand
- How to name your business
- Where to go to secure funding

- How to build a mission itinerary complete with goals and strategies
- Business plan creation

You'll also get tons of bonus content that will help you build an entrepreneurial mindset:

- Why business owners fail (and how to avoid this)
- Six success tips you can use forever
- Self-challenges to help you grow into your role as CEO
- How to deal with self-doubt (AKA the dream killer)
- Time management hacks to get more done
- How to find a personal and professional support system
- And much, much more!

You will also get a bonus Business Blueprint you can print out from my website and use as the place you store your secret master plans. This book is the perfect tool for building your very own business and it is available at Amazon.com, BarnesandNoble.com, and lulu.com.

Do+Make:
The Handbook for Starting Your Very Own Business
By Angela Lussier

17 Stellar Pieces of Advice from Those Who've Done It

One of the questions I asked all the business owners I interviewed for this book was this: What advice do you have for others thinking about doing what they love? Their feedback and experiences were so interesting I couldn't take them out of their original form. In this bonus chapter, you will get to read short stories and advice from some of the entrepreneurs' experiences as they took the leap into self-employment and what they have learned since.

Amy Jo Lauber, owner of Lauber Financial Planning, West Seneca, NY:

"As a financial planner I often advise clients to build up an emergency fund, a financial cushion to land on should employment, family, or health situations change. Now I also counsel clients to set up an *opportunity fund* so, if they decide they're emotionally and mentally ready to take a leap of faith, they have financial permission to do so."

Carole Baskin, owner of Big Cat Rescue, Tampa, FL:

Carole launched a big cat sanctuary in 1992 and has since rescued over 250 lions, cougars, tigers and other wildcats. While her story is specific to her mission, her advice is universal to business: make sure you are solving the right problem when you start out!

"If there is anything I could've done differently, it would have been to never rescue Windsong (the bobcat who started it all in 1992) and never build the sanctuary. What I have learned is that we can't rescue our way out of the problem. The only way to rescue the thousands of big cats who are languishing in backyards, basements and circus wagons is to change the laws so that people cannot possess wild cats in the first place. I learned this in 2003 when a federal bill we helped pass made it illegal to sell big cats, across state lines, as pets. We had to turn away over 300 big cats that year due to a lack of space and funding and every other year that number was doubling. After that bill passed the number of calls dropped to 160. Since then we have worked to help pass bans in ten more states and last year we only got calls to rescue thirty-seven big cats. We were able to rescue about one third of them. By changing minds and changing laws we can rescue tens of thousands of big cats from being bred, used as photo props and then discarded. The 250 or so big cats who have found refuge with us over the years have been precious to me, but if I had it to do over again, I would have launched straight into lobbying to end the private possession of big cats and skipped the sanctuary."

Darren Michaels, Flipside Erotica, Phoenix, AZ:

"Here is the problem with doing what you love: it becomes a job just like anything else. You may love it, but it is still a job. Do you want to take a passion and something you love to do and turn it into a 40+ hour a week job? I went to a coffee shop every day and wrote dirty, erotic stories while drinking chai tea. How on earth did I get tired of that? Simple, anything you do enough of gets routine and eventually tedious."

Dave Graham, Music Theory Is Your Friend, London, UK:

"It's not just doing the thing you love, but designing a business you will enjoy creating and sustaining, too. Find the sweet spot where your strengths, passions and the market demands meet. Don't set yourself up to do things you are bad at or hate doing. I'm not a good prose writer, but I can create good, concise tutorials. So writing a long book or creating a successful blog would be setting myself up to fail. I find creating fun, useful, and practical tutorials on music theory really enjoyable. Creating those kind of products based on *the subjects people are looking to learn about* has proved successful."

Deborah Sweeney, My Corporation, Calabasas, CA:

"There is never a perfect time to take a leap. If you believe in the opportunity and you've spent some time evaluating it, go for it. Make calculated decisions, but don't wait so long calculating that the opportunity passes you by. Also, don't react to issues too quickly. When an issue arises, take time to evaluate the situation and to develop a response. Often your first response or reaction is not the most well-thought-out. Sometimes people feel they need to take action quickly and respond to issues. However, more often than not, a well-reasoned and thought-out response is more effective than a quick response. Take your time and be open to creative solutions."

Elene Cafasso, Enerpace, Inc, Elmhurst, IL:

"Taking care of yourself is taking care of business. You are the business and the brand! It's called "Leadership Resilience" and it comes from the field of Sports Psychology. If you don't take care of yourself *off* the field, how can you expect peak performance *on* the field?"

Jamelia Martin and Ashley Haskel, Life Support Cares, Hattiesburg, MS:

"Surround yourself with likeminded people and step out of your comfort zone. When you are walking in faith, sometimes things are uncomfortable, but you have to trust God. If people aren't motivating you to focus and keep pushing forward, remove them from your space. You can't allow fear to stop you from doing what you love."

Lisa Hennessy, Your Pet Chef LLC, Chicago, IL:

"Write a business plan so you really know what you are getting into with your "dream" business. We have a way of glamorizing the idea of owning a business and how wonderful it will be, and we tend to glaze over some of the less desirable tasks that are also part of owning your own company. The business planning process forces you to dig deep and script your success. It shows you where your strengths and weaknesses are so you can make the proper adjustments proactively. I still use that document today and continue to update and expand upon it as my business grows."

Lori Cheek, Cheek'd, New York City:

"I just wish someone had told me the importance of having a technical co-founder on board when I began building my business. I had a team, but the two gentlemen I brought on had the same exact background. I didn't need two of the same skill sets. The technical aspect of my business has been one of the bigger challenges I've faced, and it's the one thing I definitely would have approached differently from day one. My advice for other women in the entrepreneurial world is if you truly believe in your idea, give up excuses and doubt, surround yourself by a trusted and talented team, bulldoze forward and DON'T. LOOK. BACK. And if I could go back in time and give myself advice, I'd say, "Be brave and follow your instincts, little Cheek. You can't cheat the grind, but if you give it your all, you can trust that it will pay off.""

Margalit Hoffman, Hoffman Productions, Inc., Allentown, PA

"I quit my profitable job as a recruiter in order to start a video production business with my husband. It was difficult financially starting out, but one thing that saved us was that we had a strong sales program mimicking what I had learned at the staffing agency. We realized that in order to live our artistic dream, we had to have good business sense. Today we are bringing in more money than ever, and working on bigger and better projects, and we still have that sales program in place. (It's mostly cold-calling, email marketing, and social media updates.)"

Pablo Solomon, muse-solomon design, Lampasas, TX:

"Make certain you understand the difference between doing something for a living and doing something as a hobby. You will need at least two years' worth of money to live on in addition to what it takes to start the business.

You must be prepared to work. And you must drop a social worker attitude and become an honest capitalist. You must learn all you can about everything you can. You must be frugal and think things through."

Tara Goodfellow, Athena Educational Consultants, Inc., Matthews, NC:

"Baby steps! Be driven by a balance of both heart and mind. Some of my first purchases still make me cringe. I paid *way* too much for a website and way too much for designed letterhead. I was *so* emotionally driven. That enthusiasm is fantastic and you don't make it without being passionate, but also be practical and conservative. It's all about return on investment."

Tiffany Couch, Acuity Forensics, Vancouver, WA:

"Owning your own business does not relieve you of the headaches of having a boss. Instead of having one boss (or a chain of command) you will find you have many bosses (customers, vendors, employees, etc.) and more responsibilities instead of less. Also, understand that your definition of success does not have to match society's. Success does not have to be revenue growth or more money in the bank. Success could be a new idea, or having lunch with your kid at school on a random Tuesday."

Trudy Scott, The Antianxiety Food Solution, Folsom, CA:

"There are two things I'd do differently—one is getting more help sooner and the other is masterminding sooner. Get help! You don't have to do it all and you shouldn't do it all. I have a wonderful virtual assistant who lives in another city and she is fabulous. I can focus on what I do best. I am part of two mastermind groups and the collective wisdom of a group is incredible. The ongoing support and encouragement is priceless!"

William Edward Summers, William Edward Summers Creative Projects:

"People will work longer, harder and more creatively if they're doing work they love. I don't think it matters what the work or business is because people can be very successful doing anything. […] My advice is to learn as much as possible about one's area of interest, find out what has been done, what people are thinking about doing, and what has been successful in the past. [...] The other advice, which should be obvious, is to organize, plan to achieve specific goals, and build a support team of experts like a lawyer, an accountant, a banker, a senior executive in the same field, and a tech support person."

Pandora MacLean Hoover, owner of the Think-Diff Institute in Lexington, MA:

"When I was starting out, unsolicited advice was usually fear-based and from people who were not entrepreneurial. There were many questions that began with "What are you going to do when...?" and "How do you propose to...?" Therapists are not entrepreneurial, as a rule. There was one therapist, who possessed great business savvy, showed me the ropes from time management to marketing. The best advice was her simple rule for pricing. 'You worked hard for that degree, now charge like it! Be clear and confident when you talk about your fees. Never apologize.' "

Vania Leticia Escauriza Gagliardone, of Vania and David of Buffalo, NY:

"Be sure you are doing it for love. Lots of hard times will arise, oceans of tears will fall, and sometimes the worst thoughts will come. But, if you are doing it for love, you are doing it with passion and heart, that is different. That love will be your *best friend,* and that love will always take you in the right direction. It is also very important to respect the process of time. We can't rush time, but at the same time, we can't stop until something better comes. Somehow, there is "Perfect Timing," and that is when things happen. My perfect time is now, and I wouldn't change a thing."

Acknowledgements

Compared to my first book, writing this one required so many more hands in order to make it come together. I was anticipating the same experience but realized I had become a different person than I was six years ago and needed to approach it differently. I have a lot of people to thank for keeping me on the ball and pushing me to continue to make the book better, even when I thought I had already given it my all.

First and foremost, I need to thank Mo Lotman who did the bulk of the editing. His caring and keen insight, thoughtful direction, and (sometimes hilarious) observations of my writing were invaluable to the final product. I became an improved writer through his feedback and couldn't have worked with a better person. Secondly, a huge thank you to Nick Rattner, my husband, teacher, and sometimes editor, who wouldn't let me quit. His reminders to cut out the fluffy stuff and be myself helped create a set of books I am very proud of.

Huge thank you to the following people who had a hand in the creation:
María José Giménez: Copyediting and review.
Claudia Gere: Initial consultation and overall direction.

Sara DiNuovo: Broaching the idea to rewrite my first book, which somehow led to this book.

Martha Johnson: Ongoing mentorship, leadership, and laughs about our parallel work habits.

Barbara Hodge: Formatting, layout, and design.

Contributors: I am honored to be trusted with your stories.

Holyoke Public Library, The Roost, Panera, Starbucks, and my porch: Amazing writing spaces and inspiring energy.

My family: For constantly asking and making sure I wasn't quitting. You guys are awesome!

My cats: For sitting on my keyboard and letting me know when it was time to stop writing for the day.

Most of all, I want to thank entrepreneurs everywhere. Your courage, determination, and will power inspire me every day. Thank you for all you do.

Contributors

Amy Jo Lauber, Lauber Financial Planning
www.lauberfinancialplanning.com
@amyjolauber

Brigit Esselmont, Biddy Tarot
www.biddytarot.com
@biddytarot

Carole Baskin, Big Cat Rescue
www.bigcatrescue.org
@BigCatRescue

Chris Landry, Landry Communications
www.christopherlandry.com
@celandry

Cody McLain, Mind Hack
www.mindhack.com

Craig Wolfe, CelebriDucks & Cocoa Canard
www.celebriducks.com www.cocoacanard.com
@Celebriducks @ CocoaCanard

Darren Michaels
www.flipside-erotica.com
@DarrenMichaels

Dave Graham, Music Theory Is Your Friend
http://musictheoryisyourfriend.com/
@davegrahamblog

Deborah Sweeney, My Corporation
www.mycorporation.com
@MyCorporation

Elene Cafasso, Enerpace, Inc.
www.enerpace.com
@Enerpace

Elizabeth Fife, Batter & Cream
www.batterandcream.com
@BatterandCream

Jake Van Loon, Pulp Culture
www.pulpculturemusic.com
@PulpCulture2

Jamelia Martin & Ashley Haskel, Life Support Cares
Lifesupportcares.wix.com/lifesupportcares
@LifeSupportCare

Karin Hurt, Let's Grow Leaders
http://letsgrowleaders.com
@letsgrowleaders

Kristina Villarini, Villarini Maclean
www.villarinimaclean.com
@thisisVM

Lisa Hennessey, Your Pet Chef
www.yourpetchef.com
@yourpetchef

Lisa Marie Latino, Long Shot Productions
www.longshotproductions.tv
@LongShotProd

Lori Cheek, Cheek'd
Http://cheekd.com
@cheekd @loricheeknyc

Marc Renson, Ambition Bistro
www.ambitionbistro.com

Margalit Hoffman, Hoffman Productions, Inc.
www.shmuelhoffman.com
@margalit

Michelle Dale, Virtual Miss Friday (VMF Ltd)
www.virtualmissfriday.com
@Miss_Friday

Nadine Sabulsky, The Naked Life Coach™
www.thenakedlifecoach.com
@nakedlifecoach

Nicole Tate, Media In Action
www.mediainaction.com
@MediaInAction

Pablo Solomon, musee-solomon design
www.pablosolomon.com

Pandora MacLean-Hoover, Think-Diff Institute
www.think-diff.com

Robyn Spady, Spady Studios
www.spadystudios.com
@RobynSpady

Tammy Gunn, LIVE OUT LOUD Movement
www.liveoutloudmovement.com
@liveoutloudmove

Tara Goodfellow, Athena Educational Consultants, Inc.
www.consultathena.com
@consultathena

Thomas Robert Clarke
www.thomasrobertclarke.com
@TRCPhotography

Tiffany Couch, Acuity Forensics
www.acuityforensics.com
@AcuityForensic

Trudy Scott, The Antianxiety Food Solutions
www.antianxietyfoodsolution.com www.everywomanover29.com
@everywomanovr29

Vania Leticia Escauriza Gagliardone, Vania and David
www.vaniaanddavid.com
@VaniaandDavid

William Edward Summers, William Edward Summers Creative
Projects
www.designenvelope.com
www.designenvelope.wordpress.com

Reading List

Beliefs:
Lipton, Bruce H. *The Biology of Belief: Unleashing the Power of Consciousness, Matter, & Miracles.* Revised ed. N.p.: Hay House, 2007. Print.

Job Searching & Networking:
Lussier, Angela M. *The Anti-Résumé Revolution.* N.p.: lulu.com, 2009. Print.

Personal Finance:
SARK. *Prosperity Pie: How to Relax About Money and Everything Else.* N.p.: Touchstone, 2002. Print.

Strengths:
Rath, Tom. *StrengthsFinder 2.0.* N.p.: Gallop Press, 2007. Print.

Angela Lussier is CEO of Angela Lussier Enterprises and creator of the Do+Make Business District, an online school and community for business owners. Angela is an award-winning speaker and also the author of *The Anti-Résumé Revolution* and *Do+Make, The Handbook for Starting Your Very Own Business*. Her advice has been featured on ABC, NBC, Yahoo!, About.com, The Ladders, Entrepreneur.com, and CBS Money. She is a blogger for Virgin.com and the Huffington Post and a TEDx presenter who inspired the audience to "stop waiting and start creating" in 2010. Angela is a recipient of the 2014 Forty Under 40 award given by Business West and she also mentors startups through Valley Venture Mentors' accelerator program in Springfield, Mass. She lives in a giant doll house with her husband, Nick, two cats, a fish, and a shrimp in Holyoke, Massachusetts.